THE OCCUPYING FORCE SERIES

WHEN YOUR LEVEE BREAKS

HOW TO PUMP THE JUNK OUT OF YOUR LIFE

Stella Gwandiku-Tita MD

The Violent Take It ByForce

THE OCCUPYING FORCE SERIES

WHEN YOUR
LEVEE BREAKS

HOW TO PUMP THE JUNK
OUT OF YOUR LIFE

The Occupying Force Series
WHEN YOUR LEVEE BREAKS
How to Pump the Junk Out of Your Life

For information, contact:

Fire Power Ministries
P.O. Box 12788
Alexandria, LA 71315
USA
Phone: 318 792 5972
www.firepowerministries.com

ISBN 0978706404

Cover design: Susan Harring

DEDICATION

I dedicate this book to my Lord and Savior Jesus Christ, who saw fit to save me, deliver me, anoint me and use me to bring forth this message; and to the Holy Spirit who has been my guide, teacher and drill sergeant.

Lord, thank you for the awesome inspiration and revelation in this book. You found me worthy to be used for such a time as this. Help me to continue to say yes to You. Use this project for Your glory.

CONTENTS

ACKNOWLEDGMENTS

I want to say thank you to:

My editor, critic, encourager, prayer partner, friend and loving husband Sam Tita. I could not have even started this project without the constant push from you. You brought out the writer in me and guided me through the confusing times.

My beautiful girls Maxcine, Mima and Bernette, who lost a lot of quality time with me while I picked on the keyboard. You guys are my warriors in training.

My assistant and proofreader Sister Wendy Watson—How we tried not to break the levee as we put this project together. Grace! Grace!

My cousin Solange Gabice and my sister Alberta Gwandiku, who prayed for my salvation, and the Oshodis who led me to the Lord.

All our staff in Southern Pediatric Clinic, especially Dr. Sonji, who bore the responsibility for our patients without murmuring and grumbling while I wrote. And our staff in Christian Resource Center, Bali, Cameroon, for their prayers.

Darcy James of Mark Hankins Ministries for proofreading and much more. You made it easier.

The many men and women of God who have influenced my spiritual work to a deeper level, especially my pastors, Mark and

Trina Hankins, prophetess Juanita Bynum, Pastor Benny Hinn, Pastor Bridget Fobella and most of all Dr. D. K. Olukoya.

To my mom and dad for being there.

FOREWORD

By Pastor Mark Hankins

In Dr. Stella Gwandiku-Tita's book, *When Your Levee Breaks: How to Pump the Junk Out of Your Life,* she makes it clear how believers can receive God's best blessings and overcome in every area of their lives.

Dr. Stella comes from a unique perspective as she was born in Cameroon, West Africa. With great diligence, she pursued a medical career and is an excellent pediatrician. Following medical school, she was born again at our church, Christian Worship Center. She has become a faithful member of CWC, and I have watched her develop into a strong woman of God. She teaches believers on prayer, how to be free from their past, and how they can live a victorious Christian life.

This is a powerful deliverance manual...a powerfully anointed book, tailored to set the captives free. I wholeheartedly recommend this book to all believers. Read it. Digest it. Practice it and your life will no longer remain the same.

—Dr. D. K. Olukoya

PREFACE

I wrote this book out of my own journey with God, from getting saved to living a life of victory. When I initially confessed Christ, it was because I was going through a hard time. I did not come to God in repentance, so I continued to live in sin. It was like no one cared whether or not I was saved. There are many believers who are living in iniquity; they have never really come to the cross where their sins get washed away. Like me at that time, they are church-going heathens or unsaved Christians. They are going through hell and no one cares for their souls. Like David said, their spirits are overwhelmed, and they don't know why things are not working. The devil has laid a snare for them, but they don't know how to fight back and be victorious.

There are so many believers who are hurting and living in bondage, and their souls are crying out:

"Teach me to be safe. Help me to stand. Give me the ammunition I need to fight back. Teach me how to live in this world and not be of this world. Teach me the ABCs of this battle. I want to live and not die; I want life and life more abundantly. If you tell me that all I have to do is send you $50 to get healed and become prosperous, also teach me how to keep my healing or my prosperity. Teach me to pump the junk out of my life and mend the holes in my leaky basket. My faith will fail if I lose my blessing one more time."

This book is a guide to spiritual recovery from the catastrophic "hurricanes" which can occur in the lives of believers. Read it and your life will never be the same.

INTRODUCTION

The word "occupy" is defined as: *taking hold, possession or control of something or some place, usually for a period of time determined by the occupier's resources and ability.*

And he called his ten servants, and delivered them ten pounds, and said unto them, Occupy till I come.   Luke 19:13

Christians have to recognize that we have been commissioned to be the occupying force in a war zone in which Jesus is the victor and the devil is the loser. The war was fought over two thousand years ago. After Jesus won the war, He left us here as the occupying force, to maintain and enforce His commands until His return to reign on earth for the millennium. However, our instructions did not end there. In addition to maintaining the peace and enforcing Jesus' commands, we were instructed to go into the nations and make disciples. He did not say which men to go and make disciples of. He used the word "men" generally to include everyone, even sons of His archenemy, the devil. Even though we are occupying the land and maintaining the peace, we are commissioned to preach to everybody, including the enemy.

And he said unto them, Go ye into all the world, and preach the gospel to every creature. He that believeth and is baptized shall be saved; but he that believeth not shall be damned. And these signs shall follow them that believe; In my name shall they cast out devils; they shall speak with new tongues; they shall take up serpents; and if they drink any deadly thing, it shall not hurt them; they shall lay hands on the sick, and they shall recover. Mark 16:15-18

Once again Christ did not stop there. He also said that while we were here occupying the land and winning more people for His kingdom, He would do the following for us:

1. Prepare a place for us to live with Him for all eternity.
2. Come back to take us with Him.

Let not your heart be troubled: ye believe in God, believe also in me. In my Father's house are many mansions: if it were not so, I would have told you. I go to prepare a place for you. And if I go and prepare a place for you, I will come again, and receive you unto myself; that where I am, there ye may be also. John 14:1-3

And, He gave us ALL power to carry out our task effectively and efficiently .

Notice here that the Word does not say that Jesus gave us "some" power, but that He gave us ALL power. See Matthew 28:18.

Behold, I give unto you power to tread on serpents and scor-
pions, and over all the power of the enemy: and nothing shall
by any means hurt you. Luke 10:19

If we are the occupying force and all power has been given to us, why are so many Christians still living a life of bondage? Why are we tithing and still living in poverty or lack? Why have some of our children, who were raised up in church, abandoned the Christian walk to join the camp of the enemy? Why do Christians continue to be sick and depressed? Why does it seem as though the enemy has all the power instead of Christians? It seems to me that the devil is sitting on a lot of Christians.

For some time now I have been praying and crying to the Lord to give me the wisdom to get this message across in a way that will grab the understanding of Christians. So many people are singing and dancing in our churches, proclaiming that the devil is under their feet. I can't help but wonder if there is much truth in their songs. So I asked the Lord: "Jesus, Your Word says we have the devil under our feet. Why then are most believers still being tossed around? Why does it seem to me that the devil has turned into a pair of rollerblades and is rolling many Christians down Poverty Lane, Sickness Street, Divorce Avenue and numerous other undesirable destinations? **Why are we, as children of the Most High God, still plagued by the same things Jesus redeemed us from?** Why do a lot of believers seem to believe God for things every day yet continue to suffer in lack and unanswered prayers?"

When I didn't get answers to my questions, I continued with more questions. I asked the Lord further:

"If You gave us all power and commissioned us to go to the world and preach Your gospel, we are acting essentially like the American forces occupying Iraq after the war was already won. While awaiting Your return, shouldn't we be waiting in the victory that You had already secured for us? Is there something we are not doing right? What must we do to properly occupy the land while we wait for Your return? What can I do to live my life victoriously?

"I support my church with my time, in prayer and financially. I teach a Sunday school class at my church. I do good works and sow financially in several ministries worldwide on a monthly basis. I tell people about You all the time. I even win souls for Your kingdom. What then is going on, Lord? There are multitudes like me, yet we continue to live short of the victory that Your Word promises."

The Lord finally answered me. He took me through a series of rules which I have named the "Rules of Occupation." I believe that all those who understand these rules in their hearts, and not merely in their heads, will be able to live manifestly victorious lives and not continue to be golf balls for the devil.

CHAPTER ONE

YOU ARE SAVED. NOW WHAT?

When you get saved, the Bible says you are a new creation. "You are in Christ," as my pastor says, "with new genetics. The old, sinful, messed up person has passed away and you now have a new spirit born in love."

> *Therefore if any man be in Christ, he is a new creature: old things are passed away; behold, all things are become new.*
>
> 2 Cor. 5:17

You no longer have the Adamic, sinful nature but you are new. It is also true that even though your spirit is born again, your body (flesh) and your mind and thinking (soul) did not get born again. You did not suddenly become Jewish and sprout a long beard since Christ was a Jew. Nor did your mind suddenly become heavenly, possessing all knowledge of scripture and goodness. In fact, if you had a mortgage or job, you still had to go to work the next day and pay your mortgage, gas, light and phone bills, etc. You still lived in this world. The Bible says our bodies are going to be totally transformed later, as seen in the following scripture:

> *Behold, I shew you a mystery; We shall not all sleep, but we shall all be changed, in a moment, in the twinkling of an eye, at the last trump: for the trumpet shall sound, and the dead shall be raised incorruptible, and we shall be changed. For this corruptible must put on incorruption, and this mortal must put on immortality.* 1 Cor. 15:51-53

For now, until we meet Jesus, we have to do two things: renew our minds, and kill our flesh. The latter, brothers and sisters, has always been a battle.

> *And be not conformed to this world: but be ye transformed by the renewing of your mind, that ye may prove what is that good, and acceptable, and perfect, will of God.* Rom. 12:2

The mind is the sphere of our thinking. Webster's dictionary defines the mind as: *The element or complex of elements in an individual that feels, perceives, thinks, wills, and especially reasons.* Our mind is the part of our being that governs our reasoning and emotions. God knew that our thinking was messed up after the fall of man, so He asked us to renew our minds using His Word because we are what we think. There is a choice here that we make consciously.

For as he thinketh in his heart, so is he.   Prov. 23:7

The Word of God has the power to change our thinking from its self-destructive tendencies to productive modes of thinking. The Word of God also declares that if we know the truth, it will set us free.

CHAPTER TWO

THE RULES OF OCCUPATION

Rule 1

You must love the Lord your God with all your heart, all your soul, all your strength, and all your mind. And, love your neighbor as yourself. Luke 10:27 NLT

In this passage, all the laws of the Old Testament were fulfilled. How? Well, if you love God, you will spend time with Him and you will be able to keep His commandments.

I am reminded of an analogy given by a man of God who was preaching on television recently. He talked about driving his luxury sedan on a Dallas freeway one day, after a fulfilling day. He was happy with himself and contemplating the goodness of God in his life when suddenly, in the corner of his eye, he caught sight of a police patrol car cruising at about the same speed next to him. Up to that time he had been unconsciously pressing on the gas with his right foot without much concern for anything. He then switched from pressing on the gas pedal to tapping on the brake pedal! He said further that, as long as the police vehicle cruised next to him, he remained very alert of his surroundings, checking to make sure his seatbelt was fastened and that he was driving within the speed limit. He even checked his rearview mirror to make sure there was a safe distance between his car and the one behind him. His heightened awareness of his surroundings lasted until the police cruiser's sirens came on suddenly, and it sped off in the distance. He then took a deep breath, noticed that his right foot was back on the gas pedal as though it had a mind of its own, and that it seemed as though every car around him appeared to be slowing down.

The truth is that they weren't. He had started speeding again. He was using this story to demonstrate the fact that when we drive or walk close to God by continually fellowshipping with Him in prayer, we are easily convicted when we begin to do the wrong things. This happens because we are in His presence, where there is no sin and our wrongs are all too visible. Remember what I said at the beginning of this story: If you love God, you will spend time with Him. If you spend time with Him, you will be able to keep His commandments because you will be constantly in His presence.

The second aspect of Luke 10:27 is that, if you love your neighbors as yourself, you will not lie to them, steal from them, hate them, gossip about them or hurt them in any way. Jesus defined the word "neighbor" in the parable of the Good Samaritan to include everybody.

Rule 2

In the book of Galatians, the Apostle Paul said:

This I say then, Walk in the Spirit, and ye shall not fulfill the lust of the flesh. For the flesh lusteth against the Spirit, and the Spirit against the flesh: and these are contrary the one to the other: so that ye cannot do the things that ye would. But if ye be led of the Spirit, ye are not under the law.   Gal. 5:16-18

KILLING THE FLESH

When we get born again, our flesh unfortunately continues to live in this world and is subject to earthly influences and enticements. The flesh wars against the spirit and vice versa. Even though we are in the dispensation of grace, we have to walk in the Spirit in order not to be under the law, which is the Ten Commandments. Jesus did not take the law away but gave us the law of love with which we can be able to keep all the other commandments.

The Bible says that if you break one commandment, you have broken all the rest of the commandments. **So a lie you told yesterday puts you in the same category as the World Trade Center terrorists in the eyes of God.** Jesus knew that in our sinful, Adamic nature we would be unable to keep His commandments. Therefore, after our redemption, He equipped us with a new inner person. In our new nature we now have the ability to keep the commandments of God, on one condition—we must walk in the Spirit.

In fact the Bible makes it clear that those who do the things of the flesh will not inherit the kingdom of God. Since a life of victory is assured only in God's kingdom, it follows, therefore, that those who do the things of the flesh will not live a life of victory in this life here on earth and will not make it to heaven. To put it bluntly, you can go to hell even though you are a churchgoing Christian because you are not living according to Jesus' prescription.

> *Now the works of the flesh are manifest, which are these; adultery, fornication, uncleanness, lasciviousness, idolatry, witchcraft, hatred, variance, emulations, wrath, strife, seditions, heresies, envyings, murders, drunkenness, revelings, and such like: of the which I tell you before, as I have also told you in time past, that they which do such things shall not inherit the kingdom of God.* Gal. 5:19-21

R_x – CONFESS THIS DAILY:

- Holy Spirit, help me to walk right because I don't want to go to hell, in the name of Jesus.
- Lord, show me anything in me that can make me miss heaven, and help me to change, in the name of Jesus.
- I will not be brought under subjection to sin and flesh, in the name of Jesus.
- Sin will not have dominion over me, in the name of Jesus.
- Lord, deliver me from lying, anger, pride, stealing, cheating, fornication, unforgiveness, etc. (*put in whatever weakness you have or the sin you want God to beat out of you*).

Remember that if we walk in the Spirit, we will not fulfill the lusts of the flesh.

But the fruit of the Spirit is love, joy, peace, longsuffering, gentleness, goodness, faith, meekness, temperance: against such there is no law. And they that are Christ's have crucified the flesh with the affections and lusts. If we live in the Spirit, let us also walk in the Spirit. Let us not be desirous of vain glory, provoking one another, envying one another. Gal. 5:22-26

I am sure we all want to inherit the kingdom of God. We want to have life, and life more abundantly here on earth, and most importantly, to make it to heaven. We should therefore pray on a daily basis for God to help us to walk right. You can take the fruit of the Spirit below and confess it daily. The Word of God says that whatever we ask in the name of Jesus will be granted to us. The Word of God also says that the power of life and death is in our tongue (Prov. 18:21).

Rx – CONFESS DAILY:

- I have love, in the name of Jesus.
- I have joy, in the name of Jesus.
- I have peace, in the name of Jesus.
- I am longsuffering, in the name of Jesus.
- I have gentleness, in the name of Jesus.
- I have goodness, in the name of Jesus.
- I have faith, in the name of Jesus.
- I have meekness, in the name of Jesus.
- I have temperance, in the name of Jesus.

Saints, this is serious stuff! Here is another scripture that warns us about giving in to the desires of the flesh. This topic must be important, otherwise the Word would not talk about it so often.

Dearly beloved, I beseech you as strangers and pilgrims, abstain from fleshly lusts, which war against the soul.

1 Peter 2:11

According to the Word of God, our flesh, the part of us that the enemy can easily influence, is still in the corruptible state.

Now this I say, brethren, that flesh and blood cannot inherit the kingdom of God; neither doth corruption inherit incorruption.

1 Cor. 15:50

So we have to fight this battle to keep our flesh under subjection. The Holy Spirit will help us if we ask. In fact the Bible says we cannot please God in the flesh. If we let the Holy Spirit guide us, we will walk in the Spirit and will not fulfill fleshy lusts.

For to be carnally minded is death; but to be spiritually minded is life and peace. Because the carnal mind is enmity against God: for it is not subject to the law of God, neither indeed can be. So then they that are in the flesh cannot please God.

Rom. 8:6-8

We are supposed to consciously want to keep our flesh under subjection. God is not going to force us to do it. It is a decision we each have to make. Your pastor cannot make that decision for you. And you cannot make that decision for your children. When we realize this fact and are ready to make changes, then we can ask the Lord to help us.

I beseech you therefore, brethren, by the mercies of God, that ye present your bodies a living sacrifice, holy, acceptable unto God, which is your reasonable service. Rom. 12:1

I used to be the kind of person that would get angry. I'd be so angry, I would fly into a rage and throw things at people, including my staff. Ask anyone that has been on my staff for more than five years. They joke about it and are now referring to that period in my life "when Doc was under the influence!"

I had to pray, and I still do, because I know God is still working on me. I prayed for God to take out every spirit of anger, pride and anything else that was not like Him. I prayed this every day for years. I used to and still say this:

Lord Jesus, I am Your sheep, and I know Your voice. The voice of a stranger I will not follow. In Jesus' name, Amen.

I encourage you to repeat that simple prayer every day as often as you can. It has helped me very much, and I am sure it will help you, too.

CHAPTER THREE

THE INSURGENTS

Webster's dictionary defines an insurgent as: *a person who revolts against civil authority or an established government.*

In the beginning God told Adam and Eve to "subdue and have dominion over the earth."

Once again, Webster's dictionary defines subdue as: *to conquer and bring into subjection* or *to bring under control especially by an exertion of the will.*

To have dominion is to have supreme authority or absolute ownership.

Using the definitions above as a backdrop, let's consider the following passage of scripture:

And God blessed them, and God said unto them, Be fruitful, and multiply, and replenish the earth, and subdue it: and have dominion over the fish of the sea, and over the fowl of the air, and over every living thing that moveth upon the earth.

Gen. 1:28

Looks like Eve went to hang out with the insurgent (the serpent), which led her to temptation and sin, causing them to lose dominion over the earth. If you were to ask her today, I am sure she would tell you that it had not been her intention to lose her kingdom. I am sure she did not get up that morning saying to herself, "I will wander off from my husband, go hang out with the devil, get myself deceived and lose my kingdom." Note: The fact that she was deceived did not change the verdict; ignorance of the law is no excuse. So when we get enticed to disobey God and His commandments, and we fall for it, we lose something.

As the Word of God says, the soul that sins dies (Ezek. 18:4). Our lack of knowledge is no excuse. I believe that is why the Lord had me write this book. You may not die physically, but your finances, health or something else in your life will die.

When Adam fell, he lost his dominion and gave his kingdom over to the devil. Satan has a legal lease to the earth. Jesus did come and defeat him and made an open show of him, but He directed us to enforce His kingship till He comes back for us.

THE IRAQ PARALLEL

As I write this book, American armed forces are in Iraq as the occupying force. That means President George W. Bush defeated the evil regime in Iraq and is now occupying that land until such a time that the Iraqis are able to govern themselves—until the return to power of the rightful owners and rulers of the land. The war has been won but the battle still rages. American troops are maintaining the peace. It is a serious position to be in. Despite the fact that the war is won, we hear every day of insurgencies and American casualties.

God told Adam to occupy and to rule. But when Adam messed it up, God sent Jesus to fix it. Note that even though Jesus came to earth and fixed the problem, the devil still has a legal lease on earth. Our Christian walk must be viewed in terms of the war between God and the devil having been won by our Savior, but now we are the occupying force in a world that is not ours. We are waiting for the Captain of the Host to come back for us.

We are supposed to enforce the lordship of Jesus. As one of my mentors, Dr. D. K. Olukoya, says, "People will not keep the law if they know that it will not be enforced by armed law enforcement agents. Every species learns instinctively to protect their territory. We Christians should protect the territory Jesus won back for us." If we don't enforce our victory, the devil will continue to hold our territory.

Remember that the devil is the god of this world's systems, as scripture tells us:

> *But if our gospel be hid, it is hid to them that are lost: in whom the god of this world hath blinded the minds of them which believe not, lest the light of the glorious gospel of Christ, who is the image of God, should shine unto them.* 2 Cor. 4:3-4

Even though Jesus left us in this world, we are not of this world and we must not act like the people of this world. There are people that gripe over the fact that Jesus ate with sinners. Even though He ate with sinners, He never sinned. We should be the light wherever we are. We should not live like the people of this world. Just like Jesus, we should be a voice of influence pulling the people we meet into the light, instead of letting them drag us into darkness!

Jesus did not become a tax collector after meeting Zacchaeus the tax collector and eating in his house. Instead, Zacchaeus got saved and turned from his wicked ways. God is able to keep us in this world but apart from the trappings of this world. There is a condition; we have to read the Word and ask the Holy Spirit to help sanctify us.

And now come I to thee; and these things I speak in the world, that they might have my joy fulfilled in themselves. I have given them thy word; and the world hath hated them, because they are not of the world, even as I am not of the world. I pray not that thou shouldest take them out of the world, but that thou shouldest keep them from the evil. They are not of the world, even as I am not of the world. Sanctify them through thy truth: thy word is truth. As thou hast sent me into the world, even so have I also sent them into the world. And for their sakes I sanctify myself, that they also might be sanctified through the truth. John 17:13-19

The devil's defeated army, which is made up of his demons, is the insurgents who are always trying to take us out. Since he is defeated, he can only use tricks to get us.

R$_X$ – PRAY THIS:

- The devil will not take me out in this battle, in the name of Jesus.
- I will not be a casualty in the battle, in the name of Jesus.
- Lord, teach my hands to war and my fingers to fight, in the name of Jesus.
- I will not fall for the tricks of the evil one, in the name of Jesus.
- Lord, teach me how to be safe, in the name of Jesus.

CHAPTER FOUR

HANGING OUT WITH THE INSURGENTS

Along the way, as I continued to inquire of the Lord, He started showing me why many believers are not living with authority and victory like soldiers of an occupying force ought to. Think about this: **If you were an American soldier in Iraq, would you go hang out with the insurgents**? And if you did, what do you think would happen to you? I believe you would get beaten, tortured, or even killed.

Spiritually, hanging out with the insurgents is when you decide, as a child of God, to walk, act and talk like the children of the devil or like unbelievers. Basically this means there is no difference between you and the children of the devil. You walk like them, sin like them and party like them. You violate the rules of occupation by walking in the flesh and continually sinning.

You must never forget that the "accuser of the brethren," the devil, is always standing by, ready to bring a charge against you before God when you sin.

The greatest enemies the believer has are the flesh and sin. The day you confessed that "Jesus is Lord," you chose sides in an age-old battle. You don't need to be a pastor or deacon to be in the battle. In fact, your problems may multiply if you do not realize that you just chose sides in this ancient battle.

When you sin, you open the door for the enemy to attack you and seize your blessings. When you walk in the flesh, you tend to respond the way the flesh feels and thinks, and you open doors for the enemy by your confessions. Other ways of giving openings to the devil include, but are not limited to:

1. Not walking by faith.
2. Not reading the Bible.
3. Not praying enough.
4. Being disobedient to God's Word on an issue, for example, tithing or how to treat your spouse.

When you hang out with the insurgents long enough, they may brainwash you to the point where you no longer see that you are a soldier in the army of the occupying force. You may even decide to switch camps. When this happens, you start not only seeing what they do as okay, but you may even begin attacking your fellow soldiers of the occupying force. We have actually seen this happen in the fight against terrorism, where American soldiers and ordinary citizens have switched sides and fought against their fellow countrymen. In fact, every day we hear of believers who have switched camps to New Age and other cultic doctrines such as the one promoted by the book, "The Da Vinci Code." How sad.

I remember my mother came to visit me in the summer of 2004, and she and I got into a huge argument. She stormed off to bed in anger, but I, being a woman of prayer, asked the Lord for forgiveness and prayed for about an hour before going to sleep.

That night I had a dream in which a strange woman came into my house. In the dream, I fought with her and threw her out into my back yard. I chased her until she crawled out through my fence. When I looked at my fence, I noticed there was a big gap in it.

The next morning I asked the Lord what happened in the dream, and the Holy Spirit spoke to me very clearly. He said that when I argued with my mother, I broke the hedge of protection around my house. That was why a witch was able to enter my house. He told me I had victory because I repented before going to bed, but that now I must go and apologize to my mother and "mend the fence." I obeyed and hurriedly went and knelt before my parents and apologized. I asked them to forgive me and to bless me. I then started getting the revelation that if I walked out of the secret place of the Most High, I would not have the protection promised in Psalm 91.

CHAPTER FIVE

THE LEVEE

Levee, n.: *A barrier constructed to contain the flow of water or to keep out the sea.*

The Lord gave me this revelation one day while I was **beating demons out of a tongue-talking, blood-of-Jesus pleading, on-fire, born again Christian in my clinic.** Yes, a born again tongue-talking Christian. I was trying to explain why she needed deliverance, and this revelation just dropped into my spirit. Finally, I found a way to successfully explain the concept of deliverance and its need to the body of Christ in America "without getting strange looks from people." It all became so clear.

Man was made from earth and given divine life.

And the Lord God formed man of the dust of the ground, and breathed into his nostrils the breath of life; and man became a living soul. Gen. 2:7

God told Jeremiah that he had made him a defenced city.

For, behold, I have made thee this day a defenced city. Jer. 1:18

Look at our Christian walk in terms of a city like New Orleans, whose soil (ground) was reclaimed from the ocean, the same way Jesus bought us back from sin and spiritual death after the fall of man. The same way that New Orleans was reclaimed from the ocean, cleaned and constructed with beauty, is the way our Savior redeemed us and made us a new creation after He seized us back from the devil. The city of New Orleans was built below sea level, but in order to make sure that the city of New Orleans would be defended from the threatening ocean, a levee had been built for protection where the city was vulnerable. This reminds me of the protection given to us by the Word of God to keep us from the net of the fowler.

When Jesus redeemed us, He did not place us in a position where sin could not touch us, but He gave us His Word to renew our minds.

And be not conformed to this world: but be ye transformed by the renewing of your mind, that ye may prove what is that good, and acceptable, and perfect, will of God. Rom. 12:2

That ye put off concerning the former conversation the old man, which is corrupt according to the deceitful lusts; and be renewed in the spirit of your mind; and that ye put on the new man, which after God is created in righteousness and true holiness. Eph. 4:22-24

Jesus used His blood to cleanse us. You see, when we have been cleansed by the blood of Jesus, God sees us as perfect. He looks through the blood, and the fine for our sins is completely paid for, so we look perfect in His eyes. Our sins are washed away.

But if we walk in the light, as he is in the light, we have fellowship one with another, and the blood of Jesus Christ his Son cleanseth us from all sin. 1 John 1:7

The Holy Spirit will help us walk.

This I say then, Walk in the Spirit, and ye shall not fulfill the lust of the flesh. For the flesh lusteth against the Spirit, and the Spirit against the flesh: and these are contrary the one to the other: so that ye cannot do the things that ye would. But if ye be led of the Spirit, ye are not under the law. Gal. 5:16-18

And you hath he quickened, who were dead in trespasses and sins. Eph. 2:1

Jesus did not take us out of the world just yet, but He did put the levee in place with His Word, His blood and His Spirit, to defend us from the vices of the devil. He told us in the book of John, chapter 15, that we cannot abide without Him. Jesus did not take away sin and its works. He couldn't legally do that because the devil has legal rights in the world.

*And the devil, taking him up into an high mountain, shewed
unto him all the kingdoms of the world in a moment of time.
And the devil said unto him, All this power will I give thee,
and the glory of them: for that is delivered unto me; and to
whomsoever I will I give it. If thou therefore wilt worship me,
all shall be thine.* Luke 4:5-7

Jesus has the power to move the ocean to another continent
or even another planet, but the fact is, the ocean has a legal right
to be where it is, together with all its junk. In other words, the
devil has a right to be in this world with all his junk and afflictions.

In fact, **mankind, through Adam, *gave* the devil the right
to be here.** God is not going to kill all the beautiful girls in the
world just so that you will not be tempted to fornicate, or change
everyone's personality at your place of work so that your nerves
do not get wrecked. He is not going to make people ask you just
the right questions so that you don't have to lie.

Temptation is in the world, and you have to deal with it. I
hate to tell you, but that's just the way it is.

CHAPTER SIX

BREAKING THE LEVEE

You break your levee through sin, disobedience, walking in the flesh and making negative confessions. This lets in ocean water (the devil) with all kinds of junk (afflictions).

The book of Ecclesiastes says:

> *He that diggeth a pit shall fall into it; and whoso breaketh an hedge, a serpent shall bite him.*   Eccl. 10:8

We also see in the book of Proverbs that:

> *Like a fluttering sparrow or a darting swallow, an unfair curse will not land on its intended victim.*   Prov. 26:2 NLT

If you have an opening in your life, the devil will attack you and seize your goods and your blessings.

> *Wherefore putting away lying, speak every man truth with his neighbor: for we are members one of another. Be ye angry, and sin not: let not the sun go down upon your wrath: neither give place to the devil. Let him that stole steal no more:*

but rather let him labour, working with his hands the thing which is good, that he may have to give to him that needeth.

Eph. 4: 25-28

When you walk by the flesh, you will be enticed by the vices of the devil. When you fulfill them, you sin and break the levee in your life. When this happens, something will die in your life. This may mean that you lose something precious that you have been believing God for, or something precious you already have, much like what the people of New Orleans experienced when Hurricane Katrina destroyed their levee. Your marriage may die, your financial situation may change for the worse, your relationship with your children may deteriorate or you may lose your anointing.

Many workers in the kingdom have lost their anointing but probably do not recognize it. They continue to preach, just like King Saul continued to rule Israel even though God had replaced him (1 Samuel).

This book is not about beating you over the head but about showing you that the God of resurrection can resurrect everything that has died in your life—once you can identify it, repent and pump out the junk that is polluting your soil.

Blessed is the man that endureth temptation: for when he is tried, he shall receive the crown of life, which the Lord hath promised to them that love him. Let no man say when he is tempted, I am tempted of God: for God cannot be tempted with evil, neither tempteth he any man: but every man is tempted, when he is drawn away of his own lust, and enticed. Then when lust hath conceived, it bringeth forth sin: and sin, when it is finished, bringeth forth death. Do not err, my beloved brethren. James 1:12-16

Yes, do not err, my beloved brother, sister, pastor, prophet, evangelist and apostle. When you break your levee, dirty sea water flows into your city with thousands of years of junk. Continual sinning is iniquity. You know you are not living right, but instead of calling on the Lord to help you, you make excuses, like your mother dropped you on the head when you were a baby, she did not breastfeed you, or you are a redhead from Texas and that's why you have a bad attitude. You assume that, because God is still using you and miracles are still happening in your ministry, you are cool with God and so you continue in your hidden sin. It may not be a big break in your levee, just **a small leak like flirting with that hottie who volunteers in the children's ministry** or the little white lie you told your wife today. But hear this, men and women of God—He says that He will give you a way out!

Wherefore let him that thinketh he standeth take heed lest he fall. There hath no temptation taken you but such as is common to man: but God is faithful, who will not suffer you to be tempted above that ye are able; but will with the temptation also make a way to escape, that ye may be able to bear it.
1 Cor. 10:12-13

So when you see the offence coming, cry, "Grace, grace!" Ask God for a way out. You don't need any fanciful "Lo and thou" prayers. Just cry out "Jesus help!" When you see the hottie from the children's ministry, cry out, "Jesus help!"

If you don't recognize that your levee is leaky due to those seemingly small sins, very soon you will become increasingly comfortable in your sin; slowly the veil, which represents the very exclusive entrance to the Holy of Holies (Exodus 30:6) and which Jesus' crucifixion eliminated the need for (Matthew 27:51), will build back up. What happens next is that you'll find yourself in the outer court, walking fully in the flesh. So be careful if your levee is leaky, because it will lead to a complete collapse if you don't attend to it quickly.

In the practice of medicine, I will relate this to slow blood loss in a condition like anemia. People can have a bleeding ulcer or menstrual problems with slow blood loss. Their body usually will adjust to it until they find out one day that they are anemic. The bleeding has been so slow that they may not even realize they are losing blood. The body will usually continue adjusting to the reduced blood levels until mild symptoms develop. Most times the symptoms are non-specific. People with this condition may begin having difficulties climbing stairs and doing chores. Sometimes they experience what may be written off as mere fatigue. It is common for patients to blame it on working too hard, the stresses in their lives, or getting older.

It is the same with our Christian walk. Continual slow leaks in your levee will take you gradually into bondage without you realizing what is going on. You may find out that your ministry which had started out with fire is now just like the Laodicean church—neither hot nor cold.

Very soon your walk or lifestyle will change. Slowly but surely you're not praising God like you used to, you're not praying like you used to or even attending church like you used to. Preachers no longer preach like they used to, and there are no great revelations anymore. Even the love walk becomes weak. It would be easy to blame it on the praise and worship team or perhaps on your bad kids or bad nerves. I hear this all the time: "My nerves are bad." What in the world are bad nerves?

Back to the medical analogy, let's look at anemia, for example. A patient will probably find out, when going to the doctor for those non-specific symptoms, that iron pills or even a blood transfusion will be needed.

In the realm of the spirit, **call on Doctor Jesus and ask the Holy Spirit to tell you what is wrong**. You may be sent home to take some spiritual vitamins like the Word of God or you may need to get a blood transfusion with the blood of Jesus. Like in medicine, after a blood transfusion we send patients home with iron pills to replenish their stores, and we recommend daily vitamins to keep them healthy. So after transfusion with the blood of Jesus, you have to continue to be filled with the Word of God and the Holy Ghost daily. Like my pastor, Mark Hankins, says, "We leak."

Sometimes breaking your levee is really very simple. The devil may just bring negative thoughts into your head and you voice them out. A negative confession will break your levee, giving the devil legal ground to bring your confession upon you. After all, is it not written that the powers of life and death are in our tongue? I pray that you will be quick to recognize when the thoughts in your head are not really yours so that you can cast them down. For example, when you feel tired, you can cast down the thought of it in your head with this confession: I am strong in the name of Jesus. When you are broke, instead of confessing it, say the following: Money is coming. Wealth transfer is on its way into my life, in the name of Jesus.

Do not let your confession break your levee. Give God something to work with by confessing what the Word says about you, instead of giving the devil ammunition to use against you. If you remember this, I believe it will help you. Often, it is not about the way you feel, but about what the Word of God says you are entitled to.

THE FOWLS OF THE HEAVENS

One night after Easter of 2006, I finished praying and went to sleep. It had been an ordinary day, with nothing extraordinary to talk about. That night I had a dream in which I saw a large number of birds flying over the land. There were also people in the dream. Some of them were shooting down the birds, and I was among them. The majority of people were, however, doing nothing to the birds. A strange thing was happening. The birds were pecking at those who were not attacking them, especially at those people who had trash and food particles on them. A man

I did not recognize approached me and informed me that there were usually many more birds flying about in the night, and this enabled him to kill them more easily. Then he reminded me of the story of the fowls of the air recorded in the book of Genesis, when God was making His covenant with Abraham.

> *And when the fowls came down upon the carcasses, Abram drove them away.*   Gen. 15:11

He told me that what I had just seen was actually the devil and his cronies. Go figure, I thought, he is always trying to stop our covenant relationships. He tries to make us think our God is a liar by keeping our blessings from us. Later I remembered the parable of the sower.

> *And it came to pass, as he sowed, some fell by the way side, and the fowls of the air came and devoured it up.*   Mark 4:4

> *The sower soweth the Word. And these are they by the way side, where the Word is sown; but when they have heard, Satan cometh immediately, and taketh away the Word that was sown in their hearts.*   Mark 4:14-15

It was just after Easter and the birds of prey were going after believers, especially the new converts. The devil and his cronies had just been reminded of the resounding defeat some 2000 years ago.

I was glad to have helped with killing the birds. I am always happy to be of help in frustrating the devil's plans. That to me is part of the fun of being a warrior. I love a good Holy Ghost-directed fight. It's always fun to be part of the winning team!

That same day I found out from a pastor friend who was visiting me that he had received a similar revelation in which bird-fighting was the theme. My dream was interpreted to mean that those people who had trash on them were giving an opening to the devil to peck on them and cause problems in their lives. They were breaking the hedge of protection around their lives by not walking right. Those that did nothing were also attacked. We live in a war zone. So while we believers go around carrying on our daily activities, the battle rages on, and those who leave an opening for the enemy to enter into their lives become casualties. Those that are complacent and lukewarm also get knocked around.

A few other interesting things happened on that very day. First, when I got to my clinic, behold a black bird had fallen dead in the parking lot right in front of the building. Was the bird actually killed in my dream, and it had manifested in the physical? To be honest with you, I don't know and I don't care. However, because I am always on the offensive as a warrior should be, I picked up the dead bird, covered myself and my clinic in the blood of Jesus, cursed the dead bird a few times just for the fun of it, and dropped it in the trash outside the building.

The second thing that happened along the same lines was that I called one of my prayer partners to tell her the story. She sounded puzzled as she told me that her teenage son, with whom she had been praying, had seen a bird fly directly towards his bedroom window, hit the glass and fall down, dead. "Praise God," I said. "They are falling down and dying!"

It is true that this may all have been one big coincidence, but who cares? There was underlying victory in everything that happened. We were having victory, and Jesus is still Lord, and the Greater One still lives in us. Hallelujah!

Do you feel like you are being pecked at in your life? Does it seem that you are experiencing one calamity after another, like the devil will not leave you alone? Do you feel like it only rains on you? Do you feel like your children, your spouse and maybe the world is against you? Remember the devil uses human beings to afflict one another. It is time for you to get prayerful enough to hear what I call "The Holy Ghost Forecast." It is time for you to knock off the food and trash from your body and get out there and kill some birds. It's time to say, **"Enough is enough. Devil, you can't have my home, my children, my money, my marriage! I say no!"**

CHAPTER SEVEN

FALSE CONVERTS

Many Christians get saved without true repentance, so they don't come to God with the knowledge that sin is really bad. God loves us, but He hates sin. God wants us to turn from our wicked ways. Sin is the greatest enemy of the believer. Christians should not confuse the love of God with His hatred for sin. God is a good and holy God. He is a just God, and that is why He must punish sin. The devil knows that very well, but a lot of believers don't seem to have that revelation, maybe because that will mean they have to make changes in their lives. **God has not changed His requirements for His blessing, His presence or even going to heaven.** In fact, the Bible says that His love for humanity made Him find a way to take that punishment upon Himself so we don't have to pay for our own sins and miss entering heaven. He expects us to let Him help us to change from the inside so we can walk right, because if we are born of God, we will not sin.

Whosoever is born of God doth not commit sin; for his seed remaineth in him: and he cannot sin, because he is born of God. In this the children of God are manifest, and the children of the devil: whosoever doeth not righteousness is not of God, neither he that loveth not his brother.   1 John 3:9-10

Do you know that the Bible says if you continue to sin deliberately after you've known the truth, there is no more forgiveness for you? I promise I did not make that up, and it is in the New Testament. Check out the following passage:

Dear friends, if we deliberately continue sinning after we have received a full knowledge of the truth, there is no other sacrifice that will cover these sins. There will be nothing to look forward to but the terrible expectation of God's judgment and the raging fire that will consume his enemies. Anyone who refused to obey the law of Moses was put to death without mercy on the testimony of two or three witnesses. Think how much more terrible the punishment will be for those who have trampled on the Son of God and have treated the blood of the covenant as if it were common and unholy. Such people have insulted and enraged the Holy Spirit who brings God's mercy to his people. For we know the one who said, "I will take vengeance. I will repay those who deserve it." He also said, "The Lord will judge his own people." It is a terrible thing to fall into the hands of the living God.   Heb. 12:26-31 NLT

I always ask this question to Christians: What happens if you die in a known and unconfessed sin? Who was the Word referring to in the following scriptures?

Blessed are they that do his commandments, that they may have right to the tree of life, and may enter in through the gates into the city. For without are dogs, and sorcerers, and whoremongers, and murderers, and idolaters, and whosoever loveth and maketh a lie. Rev. 22:14-15

But the fearful, and unbelieving, and the abominable, and murderers, and whoremongers, and sorcerers, and idolaters, and all liars, shall have their part in the lake which burneth with fire and brimstone: which is the second death.

Rev. 21:8

What does "all liars" mean? Is it only unbelieving liars that are going to hell, or will believing liars also go to hell? Please meditate on this. Sin separates us from God because He is a holy God.

When I initially confessed Christ, it was because I was going through a hard time. I did not come to God in repentance, so I continued to live in sin. It was like no one cared whether or not I was saved. Many believers are living in iniquity; they have never really come to the cross. Like me at that time, they are church-going heathens or unsaved Christians. They are going to hell, and no one cares for their souls. Like David said, their spirits are overwhelmed and they don't know why things are not working. The devil has laid a snare for them, but no one cares for their souls.

When my spirit was overwhelmed within me, then thou knewest my path. In the way wherein I walked have they privily laid a snare for me. I looked on my right hand, and beheld, but there was no man that would know me: refuge failed me; no man cared for my soul. Psalm 142:3-4

Behold, the Lord's hand is not shortened, that it cannot save; neither his ear heavy, that it cannot hear: But your iniquities have separated between you and your God, and your sins have hid his face from you, that he will not hear. For your hands are defiled with blood, and your fingers with iniquity; your lips have spoken lies, your tongue hath muttered perverseness.

Isaiah 59:1-3

When Adam fell into sin, he hid when God called to him. When Peter met Jesus, he asked Jesus to get away from him for he was a sinful man. When you have sin or iniquity in you, it is like when, as a child, you did something wrong at home and did not want to hang out with your parents in the living room. Sin will make us run away from God. The truth, though, is that when we sin, we need to run to God to cleanse us. When we start doing wrong things in our lives, we find it harder to pray or spend time in the Holy Ghost or even read the Word of God.

I was on a plane recently and sat beside this nice army girl on her way to the Fort Polk military post in Leesville, Louisiana. I was reading a Christian book, and she commented that she had seen the author on TV. I asked what church she attended. She said she was backslidden. On inquiring why, she said she was not living right. So I put this scenario to her: If your child went running into a neighborhood you had forbidden her to go to and she got hurt, wouldn't you expect her to run back home instead of running further into the neighborhood? If she came home, you would clean her wounds, put a bandage on her wounds and comfort her. So I told her that **she needed to run to God who was able to clean her up.** Walking right was not by her own might but by His Spirit. I also told her she needed to ask God to help her. After all, the Holy Spirit helps our infirmities. A good parent would tell her baby not to go out there anymore. That is the same thing Jesus is telling us; that even though we have sinned and stepped out of the secret place of the Most High, we should run back and He will clean our wounds. But He also commands us to go and sin no more, because we would get hurt if we sinned. Glory to God! She let me pray with her for her restoration, and she promised she would go to church and read the Word.

Follow peace with all men, and holiness, without which no man shall see the Lord: Heb. 12:14

CHAPTER EIGHT

THE PROSECUTING ATTORNEY

The devil is a legal expert who is always pointing out why we should be punished. **The devil may be a cheat, but he cannot afflict you without a legal ground.** God is a good judge and will punish sin unless we plead the blood of Jesus. When we pray, the devil always stands by to give reasons why we should not be blessed, if he has a legal reason. You cannot pray for prosperity without being a giver or a tither, because the devil will remind the Lord why He should keep your money. Remember the earth is the Lord's and the fullness thereof. All the good things on earth were meant for God's children, but, even though it is all temporal, the devil uses "legal grounds" to divert our riches to his people. The devil cannot create, so he can only steal and divert.

R_x – PRAY THIS:

- The devil will not divert my blessings, in the name of Jesus.
- Lord, show me any legal ground the devil is using to divert my stuff, in the name of Jesus.
- Lord, forgive me of everything I or my ancestors have done to give the devil legal grounds in my life, in the name of Jesus.

- I use the blood of Jesus to close any door open to the enemy, in the name of Jesus.
- I recover all my lost or stolen property by fire, in the name of Jesus.

If you killed somebody and went to court and the prosecuting attorney (devil) had all the evidence to show that you were guilty, what would you say to the judge (God)? "Hold up. You are a good judge, so you should let me go." Or, "This is the first person I have killed, so let me go because I have been a good person so far."

If the judge was good, just and upright, he would sentence you. Let's say the sentence was cutting your head off or paying a fine of one million dollars. Let's also say that you did not have the money, but the judge got his son (Jesus) to come and say that he would pay the fine and ask his father to let you go. You could refuse the payment of the fine, and let your head be cut off, or accept the payment and go free. People who are not saved have simply refused for the fine to be paid on their behalf, and so they will be required to pay for their own sins.

If you have not accepted the payment for your sins, this is the time to pray this: "Lord Jesus, come into my life, forgive my sins and be the Lord of my life."

So let's say now you accept the fine and you walk free. In cases where there is mercy shown, you are always warned not to commit the same or another offence. Thank God that Jesus has given us more than three strikes to be out. The guy (Jesus) who paid your fine now takes the responsibility to make sure you get rehabilitated so you don't commit another crime. He says, "Go and sin no more."

> *When Jesus had lifted up himself, and saw none but the woman, he said unto her, Woman, where are those thine accusers? hath no man condemned thee? She said, No man, Lord. And Jesus said unto her, Neither do I condemn thee: go, and sin no more.*   John 8:10

Jesus said this to the man healed at the pool of Bethesda when He met him at the temple:

> *Behold, thou art made whole: sin no more, lest a worse thing come unto thee.*   John 5:14b

Now, the prosecuting attorney is very upset; he thought he got you, so he starts planning strategies to get you to commit other crimes. That is why Peter said:

> *Be sober, be vigilant; because your adversary the devil, as a roaring lion, walketh about, seeking whom he may devour: whom resist steadfast in the faith, knowing that the same afflictions are accomplished in your brethren that are in the world.*   1 Peter 5:8-9

Jesus came to redeem us from sin and destruction, and He also gave us His Word and the Holy Spirit to help us walk right so the devil would not have legal grounds in our lives. The devil could not kill Jesus until Jesus had our sins on Him. He tried drowning Jesus and stoning Him but did not succeed because he could not find any sin in Him.

> *Hereafter I will not talk much with you: for the prince of this world cometh, and hath nothing in me.*　　John 14:30

So our Savior was killed for us. He who knew no sin was made sin for us. God had to judge His own son and release His fury on Him because of sin. How about us?

> *For he hath made him to be sin for us, who knew no sin; that we might be made the righteousness of God in him.*
>
> 2 Cor. 5:21

While He was buried, the prayers of David probably come forth:

> *For thou wilt not leave my soul in hell; neither wilt thou suffer thine Holy One to see corruption.*　　Psalm 16:10

So there was a technicality. Jesus was technically not guilty. He was not the seed of Adam, so the devil had no jurisdiction over Him. He was not the seed of man. He was the seed of a woman. Biologically, the seed is usually from the male and the woman provides the womb to carry it. The devil had dominion over Adam's seed. The devil even forgot that God had told him in Genesis that it was going to be the seed of a woman that would crush his head. The devil was so used to his "trick or treats" that he forgot he was dealing with a direct son of the Most High God. In killing Jesus, his trick backfired on him, and he ended up giving Jesus the pass into the underworld. We know the rest of the story—the devil got his behind kicked and dragged through the streets of eternity, and Jesus took the keys of death and hell and gave them to us.

God knew he would fall for it. Devil, Jesus was not born with a sinful nature, stupid. Oh, I guess you get amnesia sometimes. It was an illegal arrest and conviction because, though He had our sins on Him, He had not sinned. Pouring ketchup on a person doesn't make him a tomato. He was holy, so He had to be raised from the dead. I bet the Lord Most High thundered, "Hey, Lucifer, let Him go! That conviction was illegal." The devil had to bow.

> *But we speak the wisdom of God in a mystery, even the hidden wisdom, which God ordained before the world unto our glory: which none of the princes of this world knew: for had they known it, they would not have crucified the Lord of glory.*
>
> 1 Cor. 2:7-8

When we get saved, we are translated from Adam's seed to the seed of Jesus, the second Adam, with a new family line. **The devil should have no jurisdiction over us if we don't sin.**

For this one man, Adam, brought death to many through his

sin. But this other man, Jesus Christ, brought forgiveness to many through God's bountiful gift. And the result of God's gracious gift is very different from the result of that one man's sin. For Adam's sin led to condemnation, but we have the free gift of being accepted by God, even though we are guilty of many sins. The sin of this one man, Adam, caused death to rule over us, but all who receive God's wonderful, gracious gift of righteousness will live in triumph over sin and death through this one man, Jesus Christ.   Rom. 5:15b-17 NLT

When we mess up and the prosecuting attorney is trying to throw the book at us, we can bring up another technicality. So even if we sinned and broke the levee, there is a technicality—if we put it under the blood of Jesus. Jesus already paid the fine, therefore we are not guilty. Repent truly and put the sin under the blood so you can claim your new family line again.

Let's say you let somebody into your house, and the person stole your stuff and your money. It could even be that you are the one who gave him the money and he's refusing to pay back. Maybe you gave him the key to your house or rented him a room thinking he was okay. Even though your friends warned you that he was a bad tenant, you needed the money badly and you turned a blind eye to their warning. In fact you may have accused your friends of judging you or being jealous of you.

It's amazing how we let the devil enter in little ways, and he becomes the tenant from hell. He sits right in our living room and runs the show, afflicting our marriages, children, finances, health, etc. God usually sends His Word and preachers to warn us. Sometimes we hate the preachers when they stop preaching the happy stuff and instead preach a word of warning about the snare of the fowler.

When you decide you have had enough of your tenant from hell, you will go to small claims court. There, you will probably get a judgment in your favor. You have to enforce the judgment. The case has been won because of a technicality, but you still have to enforce the judgment. Sometimes all it takes for the accused to pay up is for the court to send a copy of the judgment . Sometimes it takes threatening letters, but most times it takes wage garnishment and even hiring cut-throat collection agencies. In fact, an eviction notice from the court may not suffice, and for stubborn cases you may need the police to forcefully evict that tenant who has turned your rental agreement into a nightmare.

Jesus won this battle for us, and through a technicality we have been given a favorable judgment. Now, saints enforce it! The devil is not just going to park his things and leave because you got saved. When Jesus raised Lazarus, He first asked for the stone to be rolled away. He called him forth, which is a type of our salvation, and then he asked the others to loosen the grave clothes off him. The devil has been defeated, but he is hoping that you will bring the judgment papers and do nothing with them. You'll probably put them in your drawer. You may take them to a group session in your motivation class on Sunday or whenever, where you may be encouraged to enforce the judgment. Then you'll get home and put them back in the drawer. He will continue to sit right there in your living room, afflicting your marriage, finances and your children until you forcefully evict him. Jesus said to His disciples, when they could not cast out a certain demon: "This kind goes not but by prayer and fasting." So sometimes you may have to take drastic measures like fasting.

It would be disastrous if you got to court and pled guilty: "Yes, I rented him the house. I did not listen to the warning, so I deserve all the trouble he is causing. In fact, Prosecuting Attorney, it was my fault. Let your client continue to live in my house and harass me. Yes, devil, continue to harass me; I did wrong. I am a bad mother, child, preacher, husband, wife, etc. I am guilty."

Hey, child of God, wake up! Do not plead guilty. Plead the blood of Jesus! You have a technicality if you plead the blood. Jesus already paid the fine. Do not plead guilty and use your mouth to incriminate yourself further. Always remember you have what you say. You don't have to let the devil remind you of your blood line. Tell him you are now "Jesus Christ positive," as Paula White says, "JC+."

So if you were asked, "How do you plead?" say, "I plead the blood of Jesus."

Yes, you stole, lied, cheated and as a result things are not going well. How do you plead? "I plead the blood of Jesus and I will steal no more."

Your children hate you because you abandoned them: "I

plead the blood of Jesus and I am here to start a new slate."

Your husband cheated on you because of your attitude: "I plead the blood of Jesus and I am changing my attitude."

Your wife left because you cheated: "I plead the blood of Jesus and I will cheat no more."

You messed up at your job and got fired: "I plead the blood of Jesus and I will be a better employee."

The prosecuting attorney has accused you, and the good judge has pronounced sentence. Plead the blood of Jesus.

You are pleading the blood of Jesus, repenting and making a turn around. You are pleading the blood of Jesus, and you will go and sin no more. You are pleading the blood of Jesus and asking the Holy Ghost to help you.

Remember that even though the Judge (God) is your Father, He is a fair Judge and will sentence you. **God loves you, but He will judge you if the devil accuses you and you are found guilty.** Ask the Judge, and He will give you inside information on how best to plea bargain. Since you might not even be aware of what you did wrong, He will also give you the transcript of the case. Sometimes my friends and I call the Holy Spirit a good gossip. (Okay, you sanctimonious folks, don't get all bent out of shape; God can take a joke.) Ask the Holy Spirit to show you what is going on. He will give you the transcript of the case the devil has against you. He will show you where you broke the levee and how to mend it. Call it spiritual intelligence. Once you have pleaded the blood, you can now quote scriptures like:

"Uproot every tree God did not plant." (Matt. 15:13)

"Strangers come out of your hiding places."(Psalm 18:45)

"Who is this mountain… move."(Mark 11:23)

"Even the lawful captives shall be delivered." (Isaiah 49: 24-25)

As Darrell Huffman once said, the devil is an angel, a fallen one for that matter, and he has to obey the Word of God.

Bless the Lord, ye his angels, that excel in strength, that do his commandments, hearkening unto the voice of his word.

Psalm 103:20

You can say, "Sorry, devil, Jesus already paid the price for me. You have to let me go. You have to give back my home, my children, my finances," etc. Keep quoting scripture and he will move. In fact, file a counter report to the heavens. After all, it was the devil that enticed you with the drugs which made you abandon your children. He was the one who brought the hoochie your husband slept with. He was the one who gave you the headache that kept you up all night and gave you a bad attitude when you got to work. The person who masterminds a crime is guilty too, after all. At least we have an advocate—the devil doesn't.

Listen, O heavens, and I will speak! Hear, O earth, the words that I say!

Deut. 32:1

The Bible says that He feeds those that oppress you with their own flesh, and that they will be drunk with their own blood as with sweet wine. See the book of Isaiah 49:26.

You did not have the knowledge. Like Eve you did not think that hanging out with the insurgents was bad. In fact you did not realize that even what your grandparents did wrong could be affecting you. Now you know. **So cry out to heaven. Pronounce judgment on the devil and his cronies, and demand a seven-fold return!** Always remember the "go and sin no more" part, because you don't want to open the door to the devil anymore.

> *If someone wrongs another person and is required to take an oath of innocence in front of the altar at this Temple, then hear from heaven and judge between your servants—the accuser and the accused. Punish the guilty party, and acquit the one who is innocent.* 2 Chr. 6:22-23

R$_X$ – PRAY THIS:

- The devil made me do it, so I file a counter report to the heavens, in the name of Jesus.
- I have repented and pleaded the blood, so devil you have to restore back everything you have stolen from me, in the name of Jesus.
- I pursue, overtake and recover all my goodness and blessings (put whatever you have lost), in the name of Jesus.
- Hear, O Heaven, the words I say. I want a sevenfold restoration, in the name of Jesus.
- I want all my stuff back with interest, in the name of Jesus.

Recently I met a friend at the mall with her kids. One of them, who had just gotten over a fascination with dragons, wore a pendant with a turtle on it. So being a true warrior and not taking any chances, I asked her why she was wearing a turtle. I went ahead to tell her that she should not put things on her body that will give the devil a legal right to put the spirit and characteristics of the thing on her. In other words, do not wear the accursed thing or bring it into your house. I told her a turtle was slow, and sluggishness should not be a characteristic that she should want. She and her siblings started asking me questions, and by the time we were done, I had given them some great warrior principles. In fact, I told them why the blood of Jesus is such a powerful weapon. It was quite an intense discussion. I told them how I plead the blood at the slightest provocation, which I am sure is very annoying to the devil. If I hit my foot, or choke on water, or get a mild fright, or bite my tongue while eating I don't say "darn!" or any other fanciful four-letter word. I say, "Blood of Jesus!" That way the possibility of any "arrow by day" or spiritual prankster being responsible is taken care of. I later ran into one of the girls at another store, and coming up behind her, I said, "Boo!" She immediately said, "Blood of Jesus!" Fast learner, I chuckled.

Usually I would cover myself with the blood of Jesus after that kind of a lecture. In fact, I should have prayed, but I was in the mall shopping with five children, four of them girls! When we got near a counter, I picked up a few articles and tried on a jacket. At that point I laid down my purse on a display table.

There was no reason for anybody around there to pick up the purse, but within five minutes it was gone! I alerted the cashier who, together with a sales agent and my five children, looked all over the store for the purse. My 18 year old actually remembered seeing it on the table. I lost it and started ranting:

"I am a tithing Christian. I have a covenant with God. He rebukes the devourer for my sake. Devil, you have no business enticing anybody to pick up my purse." I said, "Lord, release terrifying noises like you did for the Syrian camp to chase the person to bring my purse back, in the name of Jesus. They will find no peace or rest until they bring it back, in the name of Jesus. I want it back intact!"

I agreed for them to call the police and make a report, but I knew my purse was coming back. Of course by now the cashier, who was looking at me weird, had called the manager who happened to be a believer and knew about tithing. I overheard him tell the young, embarrassed Caucasian teenager with a bright red face to let him handle the situation. So I told him why I knew my purse was coming back and why I was not taking "no" for an answer.

"I am not directing this to you, Sir, but to those demons who dared to entice somebody to touch my purse." I released a few other weapons like hornets, bees, locusts and some angels, too. I had no business with whoever took it. I knew I was wrestling not against flesh and blood. I just asked the devil to return my purse. The next day was Sunday and, of course, promptly on Monday an associate called to let me know that the purse was brought back. It had been picked up in a section of the store I had not even gone to that day. It even had the $26 change that had been in it. People might say, "Yeah it happens all the time," but I say my God moved and terrified the devil and his cronies to bring back my stuff. I know I did not pray, but the devil had to be reminded that he doesn't take my stuff. I am a tither. Yes, he formed his weapon, but it did not prosper against me.

The devil, the accuser of the brethren, stands before God day and night accusing us.

And I heard a loud voice saying in heaven, Now is come salvation, and strength, and the kingdom of our God, and the power of his Christ: for the accuser of our brethren is cast down, which accused them before our God day and night.

Rev. 12:10

He could accuse and resist Joshua the high priest because he had on filthy garments, which indicates sin. After his cleansing, God told him that He would give him authority over His temple if Joshua walked right. So it's not just the forgiveness and cleansing, but also the walking right, which enables you to live victoriously.

And he shewed me Joshua the high priest standing before the angel of the Lord, and Satan standing at his right hand to resist him. And the Lord said unto Satan, The Lord rebuke thee, O Satan; even the Lord that hath chosen Jerusalem rebuke thee: is not this a brand plucked out of the fire? Now Joshua was clothed with filthy garments, and stood before the angel. And he answered and spake unto those that stood before him, saying, Take away the filthy garments from him. And unto him he said, Behold, I have caused thine iniquity to pass from thee, and I will clothe thee with change of raiment. And the angel of the Lord protested unto Joshua, saying, Thus saith the Lord of hosts; If thou wilt walk in my ways, and if thou wilt keep my charge, then thou shalt also judge my house, and shalt also keep my courts, and I will give thee places to walk among these that stand by. Zech. 3:1-7

CHAPTER NINE

SIN HINDERS OUR BLESSINGS

I cannot overemphasize the importance of walking right. If we, as believers, can understand this, we will live more victorious lives and be more effective witnesses. The devil doesn't want us blessed because it will show unbelievers that Christianity does work. We help him by walking right into his traps and giving him the ammunition he needs to achieve his purpose. **His weapons will always be formed against us but they will not prosper, if, and only if, we are the servants of God and our righteousness is of God.** See Isaiah 54:17.

> *Therefore, since we are surrounded by such a huge crowd of witnesses to the life of faith, let us strip off every weight that slows us down, especially the sin that so easily hinders our progress.* Heb. 12:10

It is easy to attend a conference and get a blessing, or get prayed for and get a temporary shower. However, if we are going to stop being baskets filled with holes, we need to consider our ways. We need to retain our blessings. The Holy Spirit is just waiting to help our weaknesses and keep us safe. Just ask.

The Bible says if you dwell in the secret place of the Most High, you will abide under the shadow of the Almighty. When you step out of that secret place, you need to recognize it so you can run back under protection; if not, you are on your own. We as believers should realize that sin is not only offensive to God, but it opens the door for the devil to take our blessings and put yokes on us. Especially those of us who are doing the work of God have to live right.

When I read the story of Moses in the wilderness, I found two things that frightened me and made me understand why Paul said he had to be careful so that he didn't become a castaway after he had preached.

But I keep under my body, and bring it into subjection: lest that by any means, when I have preached to others, I myself should be a castaway. 1 Cor. 9:27

Moses and Zipporah

And it came to pass by the way in the inn, that the Lord met him, and sought to kill him. Then Zipporah took a sharp stone, and cut off the foreskin of her son, and cast it at his feet, and said, Surely a bloody husband art thou to me. So he let him go: then she said, A bloody husband thou art, because of the circumcision. Exodus 4:24-26

God had called and sent Moses to Egypt but was going to kill him anyway. I am sure the devil must have brought up an accusation to God against Moses that his children were not circumcised. Zipporah was a Midianite. The Midianites were descendants of Abraham through Keturah, who was Abraham's wife after Sarah died. See Genesis 25:1-4. So Zipporah was supposed to know about circumcision too. God was about to judge Moses, His servant and friend. But I guess, through spiritual intelligence, Zipporah knew what to do.

MOSES AND THE ROCK

When Moses hit the rock twice, as noted in Numbers 20:11, God punished him and said he would not enter the Promised Land. However, God still produced water for His people. So people might be getting saved, healed and blessed in your ministry, but you still don't see your Promised Land. You may be wondering every day why things are so hard for you even though you are doing God's work. The truth is, you may need to pump out some junk from your life. We have to be very careful as vessels of God because more is required from us. We don't want to get to the end and hear:

"The door to heaven is narrow. Work hard to get in, because many will try to enter, but when the head of the house has locked the door, it will be too late. Then you will stand outside knocking and pleading, 'Lord, open the door for us!' But he will reply, 'I do not know you.' You will say, 'But we ate and

drank with you, and you taught in our streets.' And he will reply, 'I tell you, I don't know you. Go away, all you who do evil.'" Luke 13:24-27 NLT

So the fact that God is using you mightily doesn't mean you are right with God. The fact that you teach your Sunday School class or usher in the church doesn't guarantee your salvation. Remember that God is long suffering; you don't want to get there on judgment day someday and hear the following:

Not every one that saith unto me, Lord, Lord, shall enter into the kingdom of heaven; but he that doeth the will of my Father which is in heaven. Many will say to me in that day, Lord, Lord, have we not prophesied in thy name? and in thy name have cast out devils? and in thy name done many wonderful works? And then will I profess unto them, I never knew you: depart from me, ye that work iniquity. Matt. 7:21-23

I interpret **"workers of iniquity" to refer to people living in continuous, deliberate sin.** That really means you can be working for God and still go to hell if you are living in iniquity. That to me is scary, and it scared Paul too.

Wherefore, my beloved, as ye have always obeyed, not as in my presence only, but now much more in my absence, work out your own salvation with fear and trembling. For it is God which worketh in you both to will and to do of his good pleasure. Phil 2:12-13

CHAPTER TEN

MENDING THE LEVEE

I am sure by now you are asking, "Why is she condemning me?" You may actually be getting offended. If you understand this chapter, most of the battle is won. First of all, condemnation is from the devil as a result of guilt due to an unconfessed sin.

There is therefore now no condemnation to them which are in Christ Jesus, who walk not after the flesh, but after the Spirit. Rom. 8:1

"No condemnation" is for people who walk after the Spirit. The Lord uses sin to condemn us and bring us to repentance. The devil might be the accuser, but it is actually sin that condemns you. **If you want to get rid of condemnation, repent truly and turn away from that sin.** The Holy Spirit is able to help you to break every sinful habit; just ask Him.

But how can that be? Did the law, which is good, cause my doom? Of course not! Sin used what was good to bring about my condemnation. So we can see how terrible sin really is. It uses God's good commandment for its own evil purposes.
Rom. 7:13 NLT

When you are wrong, you are wrong. Most times the Holy Spirit will convict you, leading to godly sorrow and repentance which will take away the guilt and condemnation and restore you to right standing with God.

> *For though I made you sorry with a letter, I do not repent, though I did repent: for I perceive that the same epistle hath made you sorry, though it were but for a season. Now I rejoice, not that ye were made sorry, but that ye sorrowed to repentance: for ye were made sorry after a godly manner, that ye might receive damage by us in nothing. For godly sorrow worketh repentance to salvation not to be repented of: but the sorrow of the world worketh death.* 1 Cor. 7:8-10

Paul had to rebuke the Corinthians. Preachers should preach against sin and show their sheep that they need to repent and ask the Lord to help them walk right. Otherwise, they are leading their sheep into a state of condemnation and bondage. Romans chapter 8 talks about "no condemnation." It is, however, only for those who walk not after the flesh, but after the Spirit. If you walk after the Spirit, you will not fulfill the lusts of the flesh which put you back under the law of sin and death.

Holiness is the work of the Lord as stated in the book of John, chapter 15, but we have to want to walk right. We can then cry out to the Lord for help. Every one of us was given a conscience, and we know when we are wrong. In the cases of the woman caught in adultery and the lame man at the pool of Bethesda, Jesus told them to go and sin no more. The Lord knew that sinning would bring a worse thing in their lives. When you've done wrong, the accuser of the brethren is quick to accuse you and keep you in guilt and condemnation. The Bible says that the soul that sins dies. So you either repent and put it under the blood of Jesus, or you carry not only the guilt and condemnation, but also the consequences of the sin.

True repentance is the only way to get rid of guilt and condemnation. If you have a false repentance, remember that God sees your heart. **It is not "I'm sorry I got caught." It is "I am sorry and I will do everything in my power never to do it again,** and I ask the Holy Spirit to help me." A lot of people live in secret sins because nobody has found them out; but God sees them and so does the devil. You know you still plan to do the thing you are repenting of. As Papa John Hagee (it just feels right calling him papa because I've turned on TBN many times and heard him hollering like my father would, and I've been convinced to turn from my wicked ways) so wisely put it, giving **forgiveness without demanding a change in behavior is making the grace of God an accomplice to evil**. Your conscience will still judge you and keep you in condemnation. But you can cry out to God to help you overcome the weakness. The Bible says that the Holy Spirit will help our infirmities. Apply the blood of Jesus and pray fervently, and you will have victory over your flesh and sin. The Bible also says that sin will not have dominion over you.

Keep back thy servant also from presumptuous sins; let them not have dominion over me: then shall I be upright, and I shall be innocent from the great transgression.

Psalm 19:13

For sin shall not have dominion over you: for ye are not under the law, but under grace.   Rom. 6:14

If we teach God's grace without the "Go and sin no more," we are not giving people important ammunition they need in order to fight. It's like sending the U. S. Army to Iraq with information that America has won the war, but without telling them that the insurgents, though defeated, still have ammunition and are very dangerous. I believe they will even clothe their daughters skimpily if it will entice U. S. Marines to enter their territory. I also believe they will not mind blowing up their own daughters if it will kill a Marine in the process. If a Marine enters Iraq with no knowledge of how dangerous the insurgents can be, he or she may get wounded and come home on crutches, or even get killed. The army commanders need to tell their troops that hanging out with the insurgents is dangerous. When the troops are not given this warning, they may enter the war zone in pride because they are the victors, and they may live carelessly.

Commanders of God's army, not teaching your congregation to "Go and sin no more" is like a military general sending his troops to Iraq and failing to tell them the rules of occupation. Please, leaders and generals of God's army, give the people the knowledge that will save them. They don't need candy all the time. There are so many believers who are hurting and living in bondage, and their souls are crying out:

"Teach me to be safe. Help me to stand. Give me the ammunition I need to fight back. Teach me how to live in this world and not be of this world. Teach me the ABCs of this battle. I want to live and not die; I want life and life more abundantly. If you tell me that all I have to do is send you $50 to get healed and become prosperous (I am a firm believer in seed sowing), also teach me how to keep my healing or my prosperity. **Teach me to pump the junk out of my life and mend the holes in my leaky basket. My faith will fail if I lose my blessing one more time.**"

We must understand and teach about going and sinning no more. If we don't teach it, how will people know why they are in bondage? The Bible says that the entrance of the Word brings light. The Bible also says that faith comes by hearing, and hearing by the Word of God. The same Bible says that God's people are destroyed for lack of knowledge.

We teach faith, prosperity and healing, and people get knowledge and acquire faith, prosperity and healing. What happened to the "Go and sin no more" which will help them to keep their healing, their money and help to build their faith? We preach the "Ten Steps To…" and people catch the spirit of faith, prayer and prosperity. How about teaching them to catch the spirit of holiness, without which they will not see God?

I was in prayer one day when the Lord showed me a vision of His children walking on crutches and limping. I started teaching, and as I did so I saw them dropping their crutches, standing tall and walking about. Most believers are limping in one part of their lives or another, such as finances, marriages, health, minds, etc. The good news is that we don't need to. We can cry out to the Lord to not only repair our levee, but also to pump out all the filthy water in our lives.

*He that covereth his sins shall not prosper: but whoso confess-
eth and forsaketh them shall have mercy.* Prov. 28:13

R_X – PRAY THIS:

Confess all your known sins and pray the following points daily until God starts showing you and helping you to break sinful and fleshy habits.

- Father forgive me for everything I have done that has not pleased You, in the name of Jesus.
- Hide Thy face from my sins, and blot out all mine iniquities, in the name of Jesus. Psalm 51:9.
- Help me to see my own spiritual condition so I can make adjustments, in the name of Jesus.
- I apply the blood of Jesus on my life, in the name of Jesus.
- Holy Spirit, help me to overcome my flesh, in the name of Jesus.
- Help me to go and sin no more, in the name of Jesus.
- Let the light of Your Word light every dark shadow in my life, in the name of Jesus.

- Search me, O God, and know my heart; test me and know my thoughts, in the name of Jesus.
- Point out anything in me that offends You, and lead me along the path of everlasting life, in the name of Jesus.
- Create in me a clean heart and renew a right spirit within me, in the name of Jesus. Psalm 51:10.

CHAPTER ELEVEN

DELIVERANCE

You know that you broke your levee. You recognized it, confessed and applied the blood of Jesus. Your levee got mended. Now what happens to all the junk that came in? This is a very serious area in our Christian walk. I have heard great men of God preach that once you are saved, you cannot be possessed by a spirit or a demon. I strongly believe that, even though your spirit is born again and cannot be possessed by a demon, your flesh (body) and Soul (mind) can be possessed. If not, why are believers still suffering from poverty, sickness, anger, fear, depression and the likes of them? Let's examine the Scriptures to find out what it says about demons or spirits. For starters, the following scriptures talk about various spirits:

Spirit of fear, 2 Tim.1:7
Lying (spirit), 1 Kings 22:22
Spirit of slumber, Rom. 11:8
Spirit of infirmity, Luke 11:13
Tormenting spirit, 1 Samuel 16:14
Dumb and deaf spirit, Mark 9:25

And poverty will pounce on you like a bandit; scarcity will attack you like an armed robber.   Prov. 24:34 NLT

One day, during a revival meeting in a church, a lady started having a demonic manifestation. I was called to pray for her. Together with another lady, we prayed and cast some demons out of her, and yes, she was born again. A minister of God came and asked me in a hushed tone, "Do you know where that came from?" I smiled and asked her ever so sweetly, "What do you think anger, fear, fibromyalgia, drug addiction, alcoholism, and many other vices that believers suffer really are? They are demons which need to be cleaned out."

You cannot love, counsel or drug a demon into submission. You cannot negotiate with the devil or beg him to leave you or others alone. He is a taskmaster who never opens his prison gates voluntarily. The only way to deal with him is violently. If the devil is truly under our feet, we don't need to be skating down Poverty Street, Sickness Lane and Divorce Avenue. We have to put pressure on him. Our weight, even for the most "pleasantly plump" or "big boned" people, is not sufficient to keep him flat under our feet. We need additional tons, not pounds, to keep him down. We need to carry something that is weighty enough to press him down, but not yoke us. We need to carry the Rock of Ages. We cannot fight this battle without the Rock. He is weighty enough to suppress every demon, because at the mention of the name of Jesus, every knee bows. But His yoke is light. We need to put on Jesus, the head of the Church, and we that are the body can now maintain the pressure on the enemy and keep him flat under our feet.

Most times when people come into a meeting where there is

a powerful moving of the Holy Spirit, some of their demons may come out or go into hiding. Usually the enemy will wait for the person to break his levee so he can return and continue to manifest in his life. That is why some people go to church, enjoy freedom for a little while and then go back into drugs, pornography, homosexuality, sexual promiscuity, lying, etc. These spirits have to be cast out or pumped out, not loved, counseled or drugged into submission.

When the unclean spirit is gone out of a man, he walketh through dry places, seeking rest, and findeth none. Then he saith, I will return into my house from whence I came out; and when he is come, he findeth it empty, swept, and garnished. Then goeth he, and taketh with himself seven other spirits more wicked than himself, and they enter in and dwell there: and the last state of that man is worse than the first. Even so shall it be also unto this wicked generation. Matt. 12:43-45

Spirits can usually come and go in a person's life as they please because they consider your body and mind to be their house. We all come and go out of our houses as we please. In fact, we come out of our houses into a cool breeze when it gets too hot in the house. But if you are forcefully evicted and another person takes full occupancy, you cannot go back into that house, even though you may feel you have a legal right to the house. You may probably continue to try to get back into the house, especially if the current legal occupant is evicted or if you find a legal ground to reenter. It gets even more urgent if you don't have anywhere else to go. When demons are cast out of people and the Holy Spirit comes in and fully occupies, your house is full. If you evict the Holy Spirit and give those spirits legal grounds, they will come back and occupy. Most times the demons will leave you if it gets too hot in a Holy Ghost meeting, just like you come out of your house when it's hot. They usually wait for you to break your levee and give them a legal ground to come back. The Bible says they will bring seven more demons, more wicked than themselves, for fortification, making it harder for you to evict them. You will notice that backslidden Christians are usually worse off than when they started. You evict the Holy Spirit by not praying enough, studying the Word enough, or by being disobedient and falling in sin. Yes, it's frightening but true—you can only stay free if you walk right.

Most Christians consider backsliding to mean they stopped going to church. But it could also mean that they have slowed down on their walk with God. What if you were rowing a boat up the Mississippi River and gaining ground, but stopped rowing? You would not stay in one place but would drift downstream. Any time children of God get too busy with the cares of the world, which the devil has so craftily laid as a snare for them, and they stop spending time with the Lord and His Word like they used to, they immediately start losing territory.

You may find that even though you had rowed up the Mississippi all the way to Minnesota, you have slowly but progressively drifted downstream and lost territory. You will soon see Iowa passing you by, then Illinois, Missouri, Arkansas, and Louisiana and if you are not careful, you will find yourself back in the Gulf of Mexico, soon being tossed and turned by every hurricane that comes into the Gulf.

It will be very tiring to row the boat upstream by yourself without turning on the engine of the boat or maybe catching a good tailwind. That's probably why you got tired and stopped rowing in the first place. You were trying to do it all by yourself, and your spiritual biceps just couldn't take it. The good news is that you can start your engine by connecting to the Holy Ghost's power source and calling for a strong tailwind that will propel you back up the river. Didn't the Holy Spirit come at Pentecost as a mighty, rushing wind, and didn't the breath of God part the Red Sea? It can propel you back to even surpass the territory you lost and give you double for your trouble. Carry the Rock of Ages and you will walk right. Carry Jesus, abide in the vine, and you will stay free and keep pressure on the enemy.

TAKING CARE OF THE JUNK

Having therefore these promises, dearly beloved, let us cleanse ourselves from all filthiness of the flesh and spirit, perfecting holiness in the fear of God. 2 Cor. 7:1

Deliverance can be described as an act of liberation or rescue. Jesus came to set us free. Let's get back to our bodies being likened to a city like New Orleans with soil. What happens when the levee breaks and water comes into the city? If the soil's surface is sealed with heat, the water will not sink in much. If there is enough sunlight and heat, the water will dry it up and a strong wind will blow up all the junk, and the soil will be clean. A little bit of contaminated water may sink below the surface. If you recognize the danger of contamination, you will pour a cleansing fluid immediately (Blood of Jesus), and clean the soil. Remember, sin breaks the levee and the ocean is the devil that comes in with his junk or afflictions.

SUNLIGHT

Jesus is the light of the world, so if you continue to follow Him faithfully and meditate on the Word, deliverance will come automatically. The Bible says the entrance of His Word brings light. Jesus knew that we would need the Word to survive; that was why He said we should abide in Him and let His Word abide in us. As we study and abide in the Word, we will know the truth and the truth will set us free. The Word says that we, as children of God, are destroyed for lack of knowledge. As we get knowledge of our inheritance and who we are in Christ, we will not be destroyed. We will also understand our authority over the devil and how to get him out of our lives. Study and meditate on the Word, for it cleanses.

Now ye are clean through the Word which I have spoken unto you.   John 15:3

HEAT

For our God is a consuming fire.   Heb.12:29

The Holy Ghost came on the day of Pentecost as fire. And the Bible also says, our God is a consuming fire. If we have junk in our lives, the more we spend time in the Holy Ghost, the more His fire refines us like clay and takes out all the spots and blemishes in our lives. God sent the Holy Ghost to be our helper and teacher, and His anointing breaks every yoke put on us by the devil. **So all the yokes the devil put on you through your breaking of the levee or falling into sin can be destroyed by the anointing.**

> *And it shall come to pass in that day, that his burden shall be taken away from off thy shoulder, and his yoke from off thy neck, and the yoke shall be destroyed because of the anointing.*
> Isaiah 10:27

WIND

> *And suddenly there came a sound from heaven as of a rushing mighty wind, and it filled all the house where they were sitting. And there appeared unto them cloven tongues like as of fire, and it sat upon each of them. And they were all filled with the Holy Ghost, and began to speak with other tongues, as the Spirit gave them utterance.*
> Acts 2:2-4

As the wind of the Holy Ghost blows in your life, the junk will be blown away. I don't believe everybody should need the uprooting kind of deliverance. If you got saved, got on fire for God, and stayed in that fire, you would be set free. As you praise and worship, read the Word and fellowship in prayer, do His work and let the rivers of living waters flow through you daily, your deliverance will come automatically. At this level you will also be changed from the inside out and you will fall less often and break your levee less often. At this level as well, since you are tuned into the "Holy Ghost Forecast," you will know when the hurricane is coming and when to start calling on the Holy Ghost to raise the standard. Christians that are on fire for God and spend time in the Holy Ghost are easily convicted when they sin. They also become more like Jesus and fall less often into the trap of the devil. It's sad to say, but very few believers live at this level. Even a lot of preachers are not living at this level of "hookup" with God.

THE "DO-NOTHINGS"

The majority of believers fall into the "do-nothing" group. The ocean water comes in and sinks deep into the ground and contaminates their soil. An occasional wind might blow away the surface dirt, but there is not enough fire to dry up the water before it sinks deeper into the ground. There is not enough sunlight to provide heat, or enough knowledge of the power of the blood to do a quick filtration process. Because of occasional exposure to the wind and sunlight, the surface dirt gets blown away, but deep down the soil remains contaminated. Their soil looks good on the surface, and you may not be able to tell that it is contaminated until you start digging deep. These believers, though they have issues, look good on the surface. They suffer from poverty, recurrent disasters, lack of breakthrough, marital problems, etc. You have to get really close to see their issues. They come to church on Sundays, get a little praise, a little Word, a little Holy Ghost touch and feel a little happy. During the week they don't spend time in the Word, in prayer or in the Holy Ghost. **They look, act and behave just like the world and have the same problems and bondages as the world.** Their soil is not much different from the pre-reclaimed state. The only difference between them and the unbelievers is that they think they are okay because they are reclaimed. They don't realize how contaminated their soil is. Come to think of it, if they are living like the world and sinning like the world, they are probably not saved. They are just churching. These people may not even realize that all the junk in their lives is coming from a broken levee. They do not realize that breaking the levee is bad and can bring dire consequences to them. In fact, they may not even realize that sea water is dangerous to their soil, or that sin, iniquity and unbelief will keep their blessings away. These things will also bring guilt, condemnation, bondage and separation from God. This group blames the devil for everything. Because of their lack of continual fellowship with God, they are more likely to continue sinning and breaking their levee some more, worsening the cycle.

In fact, there are a lot of preachers who will go for days without spending time in the Word or in prayer and then crash-study on Saturday so they can preach on Sunday. How will the power of God flow through them when they have not spent enough time in His presence? They reserve the intercession for the church to the prayer warrior and the lone grandmother, instead of seeking God continually themselves. "I know I am definitely not talking to you, preacher, because you know better." The same lack of fellowship with God will make them not hear the "Holy Ghost Forecast" when the hurricane is coming. As such, every hurricane that passes will harass them. They preach, lay hands on people and disturb their demons. The demons might get quite upset with the preachers and might wait for them to break their levee. This will give them the legal ground to whip the preachers silly.

Due to the kind of ministry I am involved in, I have to pray "satanic counter attack prayers" after doing some of the work God calls me to do. The way I look at it, you should put some mighty prayers out there so that if the demons so much as mention your name, fire, brimstone and liquid sulfur will show up. Remember the best form of defense is offense. I have been taught to pray prayers like "…Any weapon that I have fired out that is being sent back to me should go back with hundredfold destruction to the camp of the enemy in the name of Jesus! Any demon I have cast out of anyone's life will not locate me and my family, in the name of Jesus."

Don't wait for the devil to attack you before you fight back. Go on the offense, back him up into a corner and keep the pressure on him. Your life as a child of God should be such that it should take a major board meeting and serious strategic planning before the devil comes against you, because he knows about the damaging effects of the weapons of mass destruction that you will release back. See the back pages for satanic counter attack prayers.

GENERATIONAL

When the water soaks in deep and contaminates the soil, the fruit produced by that soil will be contaminated. Some of the problems we are going through are from levees broken by our ancestors. Some of the junk we have is junk that was not pumped out by our parents. I asked a friend, who is the third generation of her family with a certain heart condition, whether she is waiting for her daughter to start showing symptoms before she does something about it. The junk in our lives is carried by familiar spirits from one generation to another. Why do people say homosexuality runs in their families? The first person that got possessed probably went through a traumatic event, which broke his or her levee. Since it was not pumped out, the next generation got affected. Generational junk like homosexuality, diabetes, high blood pressure, etc., is carried down the line by demons called familiar spirits.

Let's consider the story of Abraham while he was in Egypt, in the book of Genesis.

And it came to pass, when he was come near to enter into Egypt, that he said unto Sarai his wife, Behold now, I know that thou art a fair woman to look upon: therefore it shall come to pass, when the Egyptians shall see thee, that they shall say, This is his wife: and they will kill me, but they will save thee alive. Say, I pray thee, thou art my sister: that it may be well with me for thy sake; and my soul shall live because of thee.

Gen. 12:11-13

How did Abraham break his levee in Egypt? Through fear, lying, not trusting God as his provider and taking the "accursed thing" out of Egypt. First of all, Abraham was not only scared but, in verse 13, was willing to pimp his wife so he could be treated well. Secondly, Hagar, the slave girl from Egypt, became a thorn in their flesh then, and continues to be to this day, through the descendants of Ishmael. Abraham opened the door for his children to go into bondage in Egypt before they were even born.

And he said unto Abram, Know of a surety that thy seed shall be a stranger in a land that is not theirs, and shall serve them; and they shall afflict them four hundred years. Gen. 15:13

Maybe he could have interceded for his descendants, but he didn't. To this day, the spiritual descendants of Abraham, the Church, still have a place of bondage and captivity called the "World," a type of Egypt. Whatever you let in and do not pump out may be the place of bondage for your descendants. Even though God will forgive you, the junk still has to be pumped out. In the Bible, even though David was forgiven after the affair with Bathsheba—and she became the mother of the heir Solomon—the curse still came over David. God had told him the sword would not depart from his family.

If the foundations be destroyed, what can the righteous do?
                                                        Psalm 11:3

This passage refers to the righteous, not the unbeliever or the wicked. If our foundations have been destroyed by junk our forefathers did not pump out of their lives, what can we do about it? The height of a building depends on its foundation; that is why Jesus asks us to build on the Rock. People have to dig deep into the ground to put up a solid foundation. Have you noticed that the way we build houses these days, a strong wind can easily tear up a house into rubble? If a house is built on an excavated and deep foundation, and the walls are built with solid brick, even a hurricane will not break it down. It will be hard to put in a solid foundation without digging out the dirt and creating space for it.

What is happening in Christendom is that people get saved, but they don't pump the junk out of their lives in order to create space for a solid foundation to be planted. So they go to church and listen to the Word, but it does not sink in because their minds are too cloudy. **I am sure many preachers can testify to preaching and looking at the faces of people and having a feeling that it was not getting across.** They need their junk pumped out so the preacher doesn't have to pump them up in an attempt to make them get it. In fact, if we can study the Word, we will all grow faster. Why is it so hard for people to get into the habit of studying the Word of God or praying? Their strongholds are occupying their flesh and not letting them, even though by head knowledge they know it's good for them. Some people can be in the house of God while the Holy Ghost is moving, yet they still go home empty handed. The junk is not letting the Word get in.

We need to excavate the junk for the solid foundation to sink in. If not, we will be building on sand or just placing the solid rock on our existing sandy soil.

> *"Anyone who listens to my teaching and obeys me is wise, like a person who builds a house on solid rock. Though the rain comes in torrents and the floodwaters rise and the winds beat against that house, it won't collapse, because it is built on rock. But anyone who hears my teaching and ignores it is foolish, like a person who builds a house on sand. When the rains and floods come and the winds beat against that house, it will fall with a mighty crash."* Matt. 7:24-27 NLT

SURFACE SYMPTOMS

With continual breaks in the levee, with or without repair, the soil becomes saturated with sea water and surface ponds begin to form, producing a stench. Mosquitoes start breeding in the ponds and flying around, biting other people. Polluted trees that grow in the contaminated soil will not have strong roots and can fall and destroy some other person's house. There are some agents in the house of God who are put there by the enemy to bring in confusion and cause weaker Christians to backslide. The Bible talks about it in the parable of the wheat and the tares in Matthew 13:24-30 and they will co-exist till the Lord comes back. Some people may not even realize that they are agents.

They are what I will call "blind witches," people the devil uses and they don't even know it. That is why when some Christians fall, they cause weaker ones to say, "If that is the way Christians behave, I don't want to go to church anymore."

R$_x$ — PRAY THIS:

- I will not be an agent for the devil, in the name of Jesus.
- Let people see me and see Jesus, in the name of Jesus.

Christians with surface symptoms have obvious bondages, and they cause problems in church and everywhere else. They go home and beat their wives, abuse their children, smoke, drink, do drugs and sometimes sell them too. Some of them even pay tithes from their drug proceeds. They use what part of scripture they can remember to defend whatever it is they are doing.

I remember counseling a drunken brother a while ago. He peeked at me with bloodshot eyes and a euphoric look on his face and told me he was assured of his place in heaven. "How is that?" I asked curiously. He told me confidently, "Jesus will not let the devil snatch me out of His hands!" That day, he went home, beat his wife, and was locked up.

It broke my heart recently when, as a pediatrician, I had a case of a little girl who was abused sexually by the stepfather who happened to be a deacon in the church. The husband and wife were both evangelical Christians. The wife says she knew her husband was guilty despite his denial, because he had stopped going to church and was acting strange. It was devastating to the whole family, especially because this woman had four other children with him, and she knew she had to protect her babies.

She broke down in my clinic and sobbed. I couldn't help sobbing with her, as I realized the gruesome truth that her family was being torn apart. "How could the devil mess up my life this bad?" she sobbed. I had been their children's pediatrician for five years. We both prayed and cried as we called the authorities.

The guilt and condemnation from continuous sinning becomes like aquatic plants. These plants grow and fill the pond and block the sunlight even more from reaching the surface of the soil. With no more entrance of light or heat, the wind cannot reach the surface anymore. The person backslides and his life is worse than the pre-reclaimed state because the soil is no longer visible even in low tide. Backsliders usually have a worse life than before they got saved.

When the unclean spirit is gone out of a man, he walketh through dry places, seeking rest, and findeth none. Then he saith, I will return into my house from whence I came out; and when he is come, he findeth it empty, swept, and garnished. Then goeth he, and taketh with himself seven other spirits more wicked than himself, and they enter in and dwell there: and the last state of that man is worse than the first. Even so shall it be also unto this wicked generation. Matt. 12:43-45

CHAPTER TWELVE

PUMP IT OUT!

Now we are beginning to think about it seriously. I believe most Christians have some junk to pump out of their lives in order for their walk with God to improve. The Holy Spirit is competing for our temple with demons and our flesh. When I started going to church, I did not see anything wrong with me having a boyfriend, lying, being angry or prideful, smoking, drinking, gambling and many other things I thought were okay. I went to church and paid my tithes, but I was not saved. In fact, I took my boyfriend to church with me when he visited.

No one ever asked me whether or not I was living right or preached to me about it. I remember I really got saved when a deliverance minister prayed for me and broke some of the chains that had me bound in the world. The blinders then came off, and I was able to start chasing God.

The church counselor told me I had to read the Word and stop sinning, or else something worse would happen to me. At that time, being divorced and living a life of purity as a young woman was hard. The counselor told me that if I did not stop sinning, the demons would come back sevenfold. That scared me and made me determined to be free and to stay free. I cried out to the Lord, and He used a program on TBN to deliver me from fornication. First I had to know it was dangerous before I could ask the Lord for help. I started praying every day for God to take things out of me that were hindering my walk with Him. I started reading the Word, and within eighteen months of getting saved, I had read the Bible from Genesis to Revelation and studied several books in the Bible. I spent the first six months in cleansing and underwent regular spiritual checkups, during which I asked the Lord to show me the things I needed to pump out. He took me through a journey of pumping out lying, pride, unforgiveness, anger and many other fleshy works from my life. God is still doing a work in me, but I know my temple is a lot cleaner, and my walk with God is a lot closer, as I surrender more and more to Him. I am also living a much more victorious life since the Holy Spirit has helped me to close the doors I had been opening to the enemy by living in sin.

People come to me all the time to conduct deliverance on them. My message to them is always the same: **If you love your chains, nobody can break them.** If you are not going to stay in the Word of God and, with the help of the Holy Spirit, walk right, there is no point in wasting my time and putting you in a potentially worse condition.

Recently I looked at a friend and saw some things in her. I told her she needed deliverance and that I was willing to fast with her and conduct deliverance for her. She said she knew she needed it, but she was not ready. As one great preacher said, she wanted to spend one more night with the frogs just like Pharaoh.

Spiritual Inheritance

Believers should realize that every person has a different spiritual inheritance. Some come from three generations of preachers, while others come from three generations of heathens. Some have backgrounds of occultism, drug addiction, alcoholism, poverty and inherited infirmities such as diabetes, hypertension, mental illness, etc. Even though you may come from three generations of preachers, you may still have poverty, inherited infirmities, untimely death and other bondages still running in your family line. You need to make sure they are running away from you and not towards you.

Most churches lump all their Christians together and hope they will love and counsel their demons into submission. As a doctor, I don't give the same pill to every patient. Just like there is no cure-all pill, we also need individualized care for our spiritual lives. Aren't you tired of seeing people in our churches with the same problems Christ redeemed us from? I believe every church should have a department for deliverance, especially for ministries that deal with people from the streets and recovering addicts. Some people will need some junk pumped out of them before they can see clearly enough to study the Word, pray, and get on fire for God. **Some need the junk pumped out to overcome sinful habits.**

What did the water bring in?

So is this great and wide sea, wherein are things creeping innumerable, both small and great beasts. There go the ships: there is that leviathan, whom thou hast made to play therein. Psalm 104:25

Everyone knows the ocean is full of junk. So when we break the levee spiritually, ocean water (the devil) comes in with his junk (afflictions)—poverty, sickness, rebellion in your children, generational curses, marital discord, untimely death, prayerlessness, hindrances to breakthroughs, spiritual blindness and, very importantly, ministerial failure, to name only a few. Let's examine some of these afflictions.

POVERTY

The devil loves for us to be poor so we can be a poor testimony. In fact, he is relying on us falling into his snare so he can divert the wealth to his people. The Bible says that he came to steal, to kill and to destroy. When we break our levee, we give him legal grounds to steal our money. You can break your levee simply by not tithing and giving. Even if you tithe and give, the devil can still hold your blessings because there are many places where scripture says that you cannot prosper if you are living in sin.

The prosperity message of our generation is excellent, especially since the message in the past was that Christians were not supposed to be rich. **The prosperity message is, however, incomplete if we are not taught to keep the blessings.** A lot of Christians are doing jobs that are against God's Word, yet they feel they can pacify God with tithes. The Bible says God wants obedience more than sacrifice. If you are selling drugs or alcohol, stripping or prostituting, running a night club, pimping, or any other job that is contrary to the Word of God, you should pray seriously for God to help you get out of Egypt. Sometimes we have to leave Egypt and spend time in the wilderness to get to our Promised Land. Don't keep looking at the meat in Egypt or the money you could make in the world.

MARITAL DISCORD

Sexual sins like fornication, lust, adultery, pornography and masturbation will open the door or break your levee and allow anti-marriage spirits, such as spirit wives and husbands, into your life. In Genesis 6, scripture talks about the sons of God coming to sleep with the daughters of man and producing giants. The giants were not all destroyed in the flood of Noah because they are still found in the book of Joshua, where they are described as the sons of Anak. In the book of Jude they are also described as "filthy dreamers who pollute the body." As the Bible says, the Old Testament was a shadow of the New Testament. As such, battles that were fought in the physical in the Old Testament are fought in the spiritual in the New Testament.

Sex is considered a spiritual mystery, and that is why Paul says you should not join your body—which is the temple of the Holy Ghost—with that of a harlot. These spirit husbands and wives manifest by having sex with you in your dreams, thereby polluting your body and causing marital discord. Most times these spirits will use the face of someone they know you will not reject. If that happens to you, you need to pray seriously. Sexual sins will open the door for such spirits and also establish ungodly soul ties with ex-lovers. **Every born-again Christian who was not a virgin before marriage needs to break all soul ties with ex-lovers.** You are never sure about who or what they worship or have worshipped. Just like you can contract HIV or herpes from a past sexual partner, you can also contract spiritual junk. You don't want the devil to use your soul tie with them as a legal opening into your life.

See prayers on Breaking Soul Ties.

REBELLION & DISOBEDIENCE

Disobedience will open the door for Jezebel or controlling spirits. As a spiritual leader, be it at home or in the church, if you fail to assume your responsibilities of leadership, you open the door for the Jezebel spirit to move in. As Prophetess Juanita Bynum put it, the only way to get rid of a Jezebel spirit is to be obedient and assume the role and duties God ordained for you. There is no Jezebel without an Ahab.

When you have rebellion and disobedience, it opens the door to witchcraft attacks in your life. In fact, disobedience to the direction of God puts you in enmity with God, and He takes His protection off you. Now you become a plaything for any demonic force. **Since rebellion is as the sin of witchcraft, if you rebel against God, you are a witch.** Rebellion can kill you. We should learn from the story of King Saul and Jonas.

Drug addiction is witchcraft as explained by one great man

of God, Jack Van Impe. The sorcery in the following scripture is *pharmakon* in Greek, from which "pharmacy" or "drugs" originated.

> *Neither repented they of their murders, nor of their sorceries, nor of their fornication, nor of their thefts.* Rev. 9:21

When you are in rebellion, that spirit of witchcraft or drug addiction usually creeps in. Maybe that is why many of our children, or even adults, that get rebellious against their parents and families end up strung out on drugs. When rebellion has fully taken hold, the addict will behave just like a witch. Drug seekers will kill and steal and hurt people close to them, even their children, just to get drugs.

SPIRITUAL BLINDNESS

When your soil is contaminated, you cannot see clearly. Many Christians still have a level of veiling since the Word is not in them enough. If you pour clean water into a glass of muddy water, it will take a lot of water to make it clear. But if the glass is first emptied out and washed, it will be a good vessel for clean water. Sometimes in our churches the Word cannot get in because we need some emptying. **When I got saved I did not get on fire for God until I went through deliverance and cleansing.**

MINISTERIAL FAILURE

Ministers of the Gospel are one of the devil's prize targets. If as a man or woman of God you can be enticed to sin in a particular area, you may start defending that area of sin and supporting it with scripture. If your children are enticed, you may find it hard to preach about it. You may even notice that when you preach against something, you may be tempted with the same thing. We've seen men of God support their lustful desires with King David's behavior. "After all, God forgave him," they say. Yes, but look at all the calamity he went through.

Some of these stories, as Paul said, were put in the Bible to serve as a lesson so we don't have to make the same mistakes. God said David would not die after he repented. In other words, you will not go to hell if you repent. You may even continue working for God. However, if you don't pump out the guilt and condemnation, even though God has forgiven you, you may not be able to minister and warn other people in that area because of guilt. I am appealing to you now, man or woman of God, don't let the devil shut your mouth about that area of weakness. Preach about it. Use yourself as a testimony. You will defeat him! After all, don't we overcome by the blood of Jesus and the Word of our testimony? The devil wants you to have all these issues so you will not be able to minister about it. It will be harder for you to preach about prosperity and convince anybody that God is Jehovah Jireh if you are poor. It is harder for you to preach about Jehovah Rapha, the healer, if you have health challenges. If you have fallen in the area of adultery or fornication, you may find it harder to preach about it. That is precisely the time when that spirit may move in and settle in your congregation.

If you are a rebellious leader, you open the door to witchcraft spirits in your church. If you are disobedient, you open the door to Jezebel spirits. Like I said before, there is no Jezebel without an Ahab. **If you find the prevalence of a certain spirit in the church, check out the leaders**. If you, a preacher, are into pornography, for example, you may open the door to perversion and homosexuality in your church. Repent and ask the Lord to forgive you. It is also important that you forgive yourself and overcome that demon by preaching about it and testifying about your deliverance. Don't be the source of bondage to your congregation because you refuse to attack that demon. After you cry to God, He will forgive and restore you. Therefore preach it, so others can be delivered. Before the Holy Spirit can use you to the utmost, you first have to be a vessel that is sanctified, holy and fit for the Master's use. Before your church can get on fire, it has to be cleaned. Preach about it and let the Word clean them.

IT'S NOT GOD, IT'S US.

Most people blame God for their problems and get angry with God with righteous indignation. One of Job's sins was pride in his righteousness. I heard a story of a church where a bunch of demons had camped out on the roof crying. When asked why they were crying, they pointed down to the church and said "There, look at all those people down there accusing and blaming us for everything they do."

If as a child your mother told you not to play in the bushes, but you did anyway and got bitten by a snake, even though your mom would clean up your wounds, you wouldn't blame her for your troubles, would you? You cannot blame the snake either, because he is a snake and snakes bite. Why, then, do so many Christians blame God for the calamity in their lives, especially when they have not even bothered to spend time in His presence or be obedient to His Word to begin with?

> *Wilt thou also disannul my judgment? wilt thou condemn*
> *me, that thou mayest be righteous?*   Job 40:8

Most of us claim God is trying to teach us a lesson when we go through calamities. However, God did not say the devil was going to be our teacher. The Bible says the Holy Spirit is our teacher. **If we walk in obedience and are in tune with the Holy Spirit, we will not need demons of poverty, sickness, incarceration, divorce, etc., to teach us things**. If we study the Word of God, pray and "fail not to assemble," we will know the truth and the truth will set us free. The Word will go into our bones, marrow and flesh, and cut out those things that are not of God and purge us of those legal grounds that the devil is using to convict us. If we pump out the generational and self-acquired legal junk the devil put on us when we broke our levee, we will be free to mount up with wings as eagles.

God will use whatever the devil meant for evil and turn it around for good. Why do we have to learn through calamity? We can be like Enoch, Samuel or Jesus. We don't have to sin in order to understand other people's problems. Jesus was tempted and knew our weaknesses, but He did not sin. When He rose from the dead, He gave us that same nature as believers. He knew we were weak, and that was why He asked us to resist temptation and ask Him for a way of escape. Even if you fall, get back up immediately. The devil is a liar. You don't have to stay down.

R$_X$ – PUMP IT OUT:
If...

- Your life is taking two steps forward and three steps backward, you need to pump some junk out.
- You cannot pay your bills all the time, you need to pump some junk out.
- You keep having hindrances at the edge of success, you need to pump junk out.
- Your ministry is dry and devoid of signs and wonders, pump it out!
- You never seem to get promoted despite working so hard, pump it out!
- You never seem to find the right partner, pump it out!
- Your kids are acting crazy, pump it out!
- You are a tithing Christian but still having financial problems, pump it out!
- Your husband or wife never seems to treat you well, pump it out! (I don't mean for you to throw out your spouse; pump out your personal junk.)

- You always attract the wrong type of people, pump it out!
- You're always starting but never finishing, pump it out!
- People hate you for no reason, pump it out!
- You keep getting into accidents, pump it out!
- Money burns a hole in your pocket, pump it out!
- You have uncontrollable evil thoughts, pump it out!
- You cannot stop sinning, pump it out!
- You're attracted to the same sex, pump it out!
- You're attracted to under-age girls or boys, pump it out!
- You can never seem to make the right decision, pump it out!
- You can't stop cheating on your spouse, pump out that dog spirit!
- You are strung out on drugs, pump out that witchcraft spirit!
- You can't control you temper, pump it out!
- Always dozing off when you try to study the Bible or pray, pump it out!
- People owe you money but won't pay up, pump it out!
- Etc.? etc.? etc.? Pump it out!

Pumping junk out can be quite a task since we have accumulated stuff for years. When the people of New Orleans discovered that they could not pump out all the water brought in by Katrina on their own, they called for back up. You can look for a deliverance minister to help you. But remember that his or her work is limited to the initial clean-up process, to remove the heavy junk. Pumping out the big junk will require fasting. The

Esther fast is a deliverance fast, consisting of three days without food or water, while praying the pump out prayers. The little junk and the continual leaks can be managed properly by you, if you spend time in the Word and in the Holy Spirit. Yes, the Word says we need purging.

If a man therefore purges himself from these, he shall be a vessel unto honour, sanctified, and meet for the master's use, and prepared unto every good work. 2 Tim. 2:21

Every branch in me that beareth not fruit he taketh away: and every branch that beareth fruit, he purgeth it, that it may bring forth more fruit. John 15:2

Purge me with hyssop, and I shall be clean: wash me, and I shall be whiter than snow. Psalm 51:7

At the end of the book there are some awesome prayer points that I have used with wonderful results. They are works of Dr. D. K. Olukoya, who has been one of the men of God whose books and materials have strongly influenced my Christian walk. This Holy Ghost-inspired teaching is designed to give people the knowledge and motivation to come out of bondage. I believe self-deliverance is the best form of deliverance. If the candidate has knowledge and determination, he or she will more likely be able to stay free. God offers us a lot of promises in the Bible. My belief is that if things are not working for me, then the problem is with me, not God.

The Esther fast – The Deliverance fast
(Check with your doctor before starting a fast)

Then Esther bade them return Mordecai this answer, Go, gather together all the Jews that are present in Shushan, and fast ye for me, and neither eat nor drink three days, night or day: I also and my maidens will fast likewise; and so will I go in unto the king, which is not according to the law: and if I perish, I perish. So Mordecai went his way, and did according to all that Esther had commanded him. Esther 4:15-17

This fast is a deliverance fast. When the enemy has you by the throat, you need a three-day dry fast. When you want favor from the king, maybe even up to half the kingdom, you need to do an Esther fast. When you know that divorce decree is in the mail, or your child is on drugs, or you're facing jail time for a crime you did not commit; when you need deliverance, breakthrough, and supernatural favor, you need to do the Esther fast. Like I indicated earlier, it consists of three days of fasting without water or food, while praying the "pump it out" prayers. Remember Haman was an Agagite from the Amalekites which Saul refused to annihilate. So you may be fighting an enemy from your foundation which your forefathers did not kill. You may need to pump out junk which your parents or forefathers let in years ago. Sometimes you are poor because of the poverty that is coming down your generation line.

Let's look at the things that happened after Esther's fast.

Esther entered the king's court, and instead of being murdered for interrupting his royal highness, the king extended his scepter of favor to her. Esther found so much favor that the king was willing to part with half of his kingdom, so that her wishes may be granted (Esther 4:1-3). **There are times in your life when you may need so much favor from God that you need to fast for three days.**

The king honors Mordecai. Do you feel like your rewards have been held back? The king opens the record book and realizes that Mordecai has never been honored for his loyalty. He now chooses Mordecai's enemy to honor him, as stated in Esther chapter 6.

R$_X$ – PRAY THIS:

- O Lord, open the book of remembrance for me, in the name of Jesus.
- Father, disgrace my enemies and use them to honor me, in the name of Jesus.

In fact, Haman ends up being set up such that the king gets even angrier when he thinks Haman is trying to assault Queen Esther, as seen in Esther 7:8.

Haman, their enemy, is executed in the same gallows he had built for Mordecai. See Esther 7:10.

R$_X$ – PRAY THIS:

- Every pit the enemy has dug for me he will fall into it himself, in the name of Jesus.

The estate of Haman is given to Esther, and Mordecai is appointed overseer. He no longer sits at the gates, jobless. See Esther 8:1.

R$_X$ – PRAY THIS:

- The wealth of the wicked will be transferred to me, in the name of Jesus.

The Jews were given the authority to destroy their enemies so that the day of their annihilation became the day of their victory. See Esther 8.

Haman's ten sons were executed, leaving no heir to challenge the Jews. See Esther 9:14.

R$_X$ – PRAY THIS:

- My enemies will all be destroyed, in the name of Jesus.

The Jews were given royal protection when King Xerxes sent letters to all the provinces to assure their peace. See Esther 9:30.

Mordecai was promoted to Prime Minister. See Esther 10:3.

The multitudes had fasted for three days and he healed them all, then he fed the four thousand (See Matt. 15:30-32).

Here is one of the times the healing power of Jesus flowed to overflow, when the people fasted for three days and Jesus healed every one of them. Every time I have wanted something from

God very badly, I have always gotten the answer after a three-day dry fast. I have also had the most amazing anointing and witnessed the move of God when I have gone to preach after three days of dry fasting. So even for you, minister of God, if you want something to break loose in your ministry, you should try three days of dry fasting, while praying the prayer called "Attacking the enemy of my calling," found at the end of the book .

HOLY PURGING

We get defiled by what we say and do, and I believe that believers need to go through what I call "holy purging." This is especially true if you are a minister of the Gospel. Ministers are usually under a fiercer attack by the enemy because they are troubling the waters for the enemy all the time. So the enemy is usually looking for ways to disgrace them. Just like the devil always tried to disgrace Jesus when He walked the earth, through the religious leaders.

> *Then Jesus called to the crowd to come and hear. "All of you listen," he said, "and try to understand. You are not defiled by what you eat; you are defiled by what you say and do!"*
>
> Mark 7:14-15

I believe during the time of refreshing and renewing, you need to pray both some spiritual sanitation and "fill me afresh" prayers. You may say, "I am saved, I have the hook up, I am a mighty man of God." I hope you don't ever sin. In fact, I hope it isn't spiritual pride causing you to speak that way. You need to go to God to clean you out every now and then, while refilling you. You may not agree with me, but I am a warrior and love being on the offensive. When you read through the prayer points found at the end of the book, some may sound or appear strange to you. But pray them anyway, and if they do not pertain to your life, nothing will happen.

A while back I introduced a friend to Dr. Olukoya's type of violent prayers. She refused to pray some of the prayer points because, she claimed, they did not pertain to her. In response, I told her that if I was told to ask every Goliath in my life to die, I would pray like I saw the Goliaths. I asked her whether she could see clearly enough in the spirit to tell that there were no Goliaths in her life. She was actually a Holy Ghost-filled, on-fire Christian who had been prayer-walking her city under the direction of the Holy Spirit. She started having strange medical symptoms and was at one point on thyroid medication. Finally she started asking the elephants, Goliaths, vultures, etc., to fall down and die. She got completely healed, and now we can go toe to toe in some good, old-fashioned devil butt-kicking prayers. I am a witness because I was delivered from insomnia and migraine headaches when I started asking the enemy to be destroyed in my life. I prayed foundational prayers, combined with a partial fast for ten days. By day seven, I went to sleep for the first time in years without a sleeping pill.

Always remember you are not warring against flesh and blood, but against the devil's invisible army. See Ephesians

6:10-14. So do not pray against people, because it will not work, but pray against the forces that are influencing their behavior

CHAPTER THIRTEEN

KEEPING THE LEVEE INTACT

How do you keep your levee intact? To keep your levee intact, you have to walk right, read and meditate on the Word of God, pray in the Holy Ghost and crucify your flesh. It is important to know that it is God who helps you to walk right, so you must ask Him to help you.

WALKING RIGHT – JUST ASK

Keeping our levees intact, or walking right, is something we cannot do by ourselves. The book of John, chapter 15, talks about believers bearing fruit only by abiding in the vine. In Galatians chapter 5, it says that if we walk in the Spirit, we will not fulfill the lusts of the flesh. Most of us find it hard because we have not and do not study the Word of God.

Thy word have I hid in mine heart, that I might not sin against thee. Psalm 119:11

The Word of God will help you not to sin.

Align your confession with the Word of God.

Let's say, for example, you feel tired. Instead of confessing that you are tired and opening up the levee for the spirit of weariness to come in, confess what the Word says: "I am strong, in the name of Jesus. I can do all things through Christ who strengthens me." The Word of God is food for your spirit. You can go to church, jump and shout and say "money cometh." But if after you come out of church somebody asks you for money and you say that you are broke, you just opened up your levee for the spirit of poverty. The Word of God says that the power of life and death are in our tongue. So when you speak death to your finances, upon your marriage or your children, the devil will stand there to enforce it.

The Word of God will make your way prosperous.

This book of the law shall not depart out of thy mouth; but thou shalt meditate therein day and night, that thou mayest observe to do according to all that is written therein: for then thou shalt make thy way prosperous, and then thou shalt have good success. Joshua 1:8

It will direct you.

Thy word is a lamp unto my feet, and a light unto my path.
Psalm 119:105

If you are directed by the Word of God in everything you do, you will not go wrong. The Word of God is a two-edged sword and has the ability to cut junk out of your life.

For the Word of God is quick, and powerful, and sharper than any two-edged sword, piercing even to the dividing asunder of soul and spirit, and of the joints and marrow, and is a discerner of the thoughts and intents of the heart. Neither is there any creature that is not manifest in his sight: but all things are naked and opened unto the eyes of him with whom we have to do. Heb. 4:12-13

The Word of God has healing power.

My son, attend to my words; incline thine ear unto my sayings. Let them not depart from thine eyes; keep them in the midst of thine heart. For they are life unto those that find them, and health to all their flesh. Prov. 4:20-22

The Word of God is the sword of the Spirit. If you abide by it, and quote it, the devil has to obey. Even Jesus who was God needed the Word to defeat the devil. God is able to keep you from falling. We have to understand that sin and flesh are the causes of most of our problems, even down to our generations. The Lord will help us to break that power, but we have to abide in Him and in His Word.

Holy Spirit

I have spent so much of this book talking about the junk in our lives and how to pump it out that by now I am sure some of you are asking, "What about just being in the Holy Ghost?" I know some people take it to the extreme, and all they do is war. But we have to spend time in the Holy Ghost and in the Word of God in order to be victorious in battle. I know most of us already understand the part about spending time in the Holy Ghost. When you spend time in praise, worship and thanksgiving, you connect to the power source. In fact, before I do spiritual kick-boxing I spend time in praise, worship and praying in the Holy Ghost. When you spend time in the Holy Ghost you get charged and built up so you can continue to give out spiritually. When you war without the Holy Ghost, you are fighting a parallel battle in which the devil can whip you silly. If you spend time with the Lord and abide in His Word, your sword will be sharp and you will be confronting the enemy from above, in heavenly places, far above all principality, and power, and might, and dominion. In this way victory is assured.

> *Now unto him that is able to keep you from falling, and to present you faultless before the presence of his glory with exceeding joy.* Jude 24

The Holy Spirit is our helper. He helps us to stand. If you get that time of refreshing in the Holy Ghost, you will be able to walk right because He will change your appetites from the inside out. He will also convict you when you are going wrong and bring you to true repentance. His desire is to keep you from falling because you are a member of His battalion and He doesn't want you hurt.

And God is able to make all grace abound toward you; that ye, always having all sufficiency in all things, may abound to every good work: 2 Cor. 9:8

It is the Lord's will for us to walk in victory, because we will be better testimonies and workers in His kingdom. He wants you to be prosperous so you can foster the growth of His kingdom. If you are prosperous in ministry, in your finances, marriage, etc., you can be a greater influence in the world.

He staggered not at the promise of God through unbelief; but was strong in faith, giving glory to God; and being fully persuaded that, what he had promised, he was able also to perform. Rom. 4:20-21

God wants to show off in our lives. He wants people to say, "Wow! That is God's blessing." He wants His glory to show through us, because His glory is His goodness. Why do we dress our kids in pretty outfits when they go out? It is usually because we want to demonstrate our ability to provide for them.

God even makes provision to pray for us when we pray in the Holy Ghost. Don't you just feel sorry for those who don't have access to the extra boost that comes from praying in the Holy Ghost? I am sure that some of you have had that time when you prayed in the Spirit, and cried like your heart was breaking. And, of course, there is always a feeling of a great release afterwards. I know I have experienced it on several occasions.

Likewise the Spirit also helpeth our infirmities: for we know not what we should pray for as we ought: but the Spirit itself maketh intercession for us with groanings which cannot be uttered. And he that searcheth the hearts knoweth what is the mind of the Spirit, because he maketh intercession for the saints according to the will of God. Rom. 8:26-27

The Holy Spirit can comfort you in those dark times until you can get up and kick box.

If ye love me, keep my commandments. And I will pray the Father, and he shall give you another Comforter, that he may abide with you for ever; even the Spirit of truth; whom the world cannot receive, because it seeth him not, neither knoweth him: but ye know him; for he dwelleth with you, and shall be in you. I will not leave you comfortless: I will come to you.
John 14:15-18

If you love Jesus, He will help you to keep His commandments. He has also given you a comforter and a teacher, in the person of the Holy Spirit. The Holy Spirit happens to be a gentleman, and will not force Himself on you. But if you need to know the truth, just ask Him.

If you are finding it difficult to understand the Word, just ask.

If you need help in keeping His commandments or walking right, just ask.

When the Spirit of truth comes, he will guide you into all truth. He will not be presenting his own ideas; he will be telling you what he has heard. He will tell you about the future. He will bring me glory by revealing to you whatever he receives from me. All that the Father has is mine; this is what I mean when I say that the Spirit will reveal to you whatever he receives from me.   John 16:13-15 NLT

I remember a time when one of my cousins had hurt me terribly. In my pain I felt I would never get over it. Not wanting to be unforgiving for even one day, I just cried out like blind Bartimaeus, "Jesus help! I don't want to carry this grudge because I know it will break my levee, but Lord I feel so angry and hurt. Jesus help!" Within ten minutes I felt a peace come over me, and the offence lifted. I remember countless times when I have—despite my bad-to-the-bone warrior attitude—just gotten down on my face and cried out, "Holy Spirit, help! Jesus, help! I don't know what to do. Jesus help!"

CHAPTER FOURTEEN

SPIRITUAL INTELLIGENCE

Examine yourself daily to make sure you are still in the faith.

I have already warned those who had been sinning when I was there on my second visit. Now I again warn them and all others, just as I did before, that this next time I will not spare them. I will give you all the proof you want that Christ speaks through me. Christ is not weak in his dealings with you; he is a mighty power among you. Although he died on the cross in weakness, he now lives by the mighty power of God. We, too, are weak, but we live in him and have God's power—the power we use in dealing with you. Examine yourselves to see if your faith is really genuine. Test yourselves. If you cannot tell that Jesus Christ is among you,* it means you have failed the test. I hope you recognize that we have passed the test and are approved by God. 2 Cor. 13: 2-6 NLT*

Listen to the Holy Ghost Weather Forecast: You tune in to the Holy Ghost Forecast by praying, going to church, watching Christian television, listening to Christian radio, reading the Word, listening to sermons on tape and on CDs, etc.

Think about this: If your radio or television is not turned on, you can't receive any broadcasts. In the same way, if your spiritual radio is not on, meaning that you have not turned on your desire for God, you cannot receive any broadcasts from Him. Your spiritual radio may be on, but you may not be tuned to the right station. (You tune in to the Holy Ghost station by praising and worshipping.) If you don't have a radio at all, then you are either an unbeliever or a backslider, and cannot hear from God. In any of the above cases, you cannot hear the Holy Ghost Weather Forecast that warns of the flood that is approaching. When you tune in and get the forecast, then you can ask the engineers who built your levee in the first place to fortify it and make it ready for the impending flood (Holy Spirit helping to fortify you). You can also build up yourself and fortify your levee by praying in the Holy Ghost.

But ye, beloved, building up yourselves on your most holy faith, praying in the Holy Ghost, keep yourselves in the love of God, looking for the mercy of our Lord Jesus Christ unto eternal life. Jude 1:20-21

If you pray and are in tune with the Holy Spirit, He will show you when the attacks are coming, and you will be able to fortify yourself with more prayer and fasting. Just ask.

He revealeth the deep and secret things: he knoweth what is in the darkness, and the light dwelleth with him.   Daniel 2:22

God will reveal the snares in your life, because He wants you refined, so you can be able to keep His Word.

The secret things belong unto the Lord our God: but those things which are revealed belong unto us and to our children for ever, that we may do all the words of this law.

Deut. 29:29

The Bible says that when the enemy comes in like a flood, the Spirit will lift up a standard against him. But you have to ask.

So shall they fear the name of the Lord from the west, and his glory from the rising of the sun. When the enemy shall come in like a flood, the Spirit of the Lord shall lift up a standard against him.   Isaiah 59:19

The same way we go for yearly checkups, I believe we as believers should do regular spiritual checkups. Get Spiritual Intelligence. The Holy Spirit can inform us when things are going wrong if we tune in by spending time with Him and praying in the Holy Ghost. Praise and worship is a great way to tune in. The Bible says that we should come into God's presence with thanksgiving, and into His courts with praise. Deep worship will take you into God's presence and deliverance may ensue. When Elisha needed to inquire of God, he asked for a harpist to usher him into His presence.

> *"Now bring me someone who can play the harp." While the harp was being played, the power of the Lord came upon Elisha.* 2 Kings 3:15

How does the Holy Spirit inform me when I have junk? I start having dreams in which I see dirt or strange people in my house. Your house (your temple) in a dream will most times signify your body. Because I pray a lot for people, sometimes the counter attack from the devil can be very oppressive. Usually I feel the oppression as a cloudy sensation in my head, a feeling of weariness. When that happens, I go into spiritual sanitation prayers. I ask the blood of Jesus and the fire of the Holy Ghost to purge me. The same way that I feel the presence of the Holy Spirit on my body is the way that I feel a fiery dart, or an arrow-by-day that hits me. During the course of my day, if I get any sudden sharp pain, I backfire it immediately. If the pain was generated physically and not spiritually, then nothing happens. But nine out of ten times, the pain goes away. I have backfired headaches, stomach cramps, muscle cramps and sharp pains, and they've all gone away. I have even backfired feelings of oppression in my life and in other people's lives on numerous occasions, and the symptoms have disappeared immediately.

R$_X$ – PRAY THIS:

- I backfire any arrow of the enemy fired at me by fire, in the name of Jesus.

- You will come against me one way and flee in seven ways, in the name of Jesus.

- Every oppression of the enemy, go back and oppress the oppressor, in the name of Jesus.

More prayers are attached at the end of the book.

It is dangerous to break your levee and keep breaking it. If you do not realize that it is dangerous, you will not mend it, and you will not endeavor to keep it intact. That is why I have written this book.

CHAPTER FIFTEEN

LAND RECLAMATION

As bad as New Orleans got after Hurricane Katrina, we can now see that the Corp of Engineers came in and rebuilt the levee, and the city administration cleaned it up, even as the same Jesus who paid for your sins also paid for your deliverance. The builder of your levee has given you a life-time guarantee for parts and labor, regular checkups and even complete replacement if necessary.

But you have to call Him and tell Him what you want—just ask. You don't have to pay for anything. The warranty is fully paid for. Jesus took care of it. All you have to do is sign up for it and call for regular checkups—just ask.

I called on the Lord and He heard my cry and brought me out of the horrible pit. No matter how bad your case is, if you are willing to make some changes, fast and pray, I am sure God will turn things around and give you many testimonies, in the name of Jesus—just ask.

In conclusion, some people may say that they have done all these things and their prayers are still not being answered. Most religious folks will say that all one has to do is stand. It says so in the book of Ephesians. However, the stance referred to is a warrior stance. In fact, after standing and putting on the whole armor of God, we are asked to pray all kinds of prayers; that means warfare, intercessory, exaltation, praise and thanksgiving—all kinds of prayers.

Finally, my brethren, be strong in the Lord, and in the power of his might. Put on the whole armor of God that ye may be able to stand against the wiles of the devil. For we wrestle not against flesh and blood, but against principalities, against powers, against the rulers of the darkness of this world, against spiritual wickedness in high places. Wherefore take unto you the whole armor of God that ye may be able to withstand in the evil day, and having done all, to stand. Stand therefore, having your loins girt about with truth, and having on the breastplate of righteousness; and your feet shod with the preparation of the gospel of peace; above all, taking the shield of faith, wherewith ye shall be able to quench all the fiery darts of the wicked. And take the helmet of salvation, and the sword of the Spirit, which is the Word of God: praying always with all prayer and supplication in the Spirit, and watching thereunto with all perseverance and supplication for all saints.

Eph. 6:10-18

Verse 18 says "praying always." So you pray until God answers. Your answer may be a "No," but it is an answer. Pray, fast, pump out some more junk and study the Word. But do not stop. Do not give up until God blesses you. Take the stance Jacob took. This battle goes on until the Lord Jesus comes back, or you go to glory. The minute you stop, you start losing ground like the boat rowing up the Mississippi River.

It took the children of Israel forty years to make an eleven-day journey. The Lord would not let them complete the journey initially because they had to learn warfare, and subsequently because they had unbelief.

(There are eleven days' journey from Horeb by the way of mount Seir unto Kadesh-barnea.) And it came to pass in the fortieth year... Deut. 1:2-3

So wake up, child of God, and learn how to take it by force! Enforce your occupation. Refuse to take "No" for an answer. I would love to comfort you by saying, "Just stand and all will be well." But no, no, no! Fight until you are truly occupying and do not let go until the Lord blesses you.

EPILOGUE

I am including several different prayer points on various topics, written by Dr. D. K. Olukoya. These prayers have helped me and I believe they will help you, too.

I hope this book has challenged you to aspire to get to your Promised Land in eleven days instead of forty years. You don't have to die in the wilderness like the children of Israel, in the name of Jesus. Amen.

While editing this book, I spoke to an evangelical Christian sister who had an issue with being asked to repeat a prayer point numerous times. To her it sounded like a chant, or that it was almost cultic and could put one into a trance. Many cultic groups and non-Christian religions tend to do a lot of chanting, repetitions and long meditation to link to their demonic powers. The devil did not create that either, he just distorted it from God. Most Christians that have separated themselves, prayed fervently, and are in sound doctrine will have a divine encounter. Repetition in prayer is very good if done fervently, not just repeating mere words without knowledge. I actually do believe you should stick to whatever point you are making to God until He answers.

Some Christians are spooked by the supernatural and never get any real encounters with God. The majority do not want to put in the time in prayer and meditation in the Word that can result in a meaningful encounter. In the days when the church mamas lay on the altar and said, "Move in this place, Lord" for hours, the Lord moved meaningfully, with signs and wonders following.

Our Savior Himself gave us a great example of repeating a prayer point as He labored in the Garden of Gethsemane. He said three times in Matthew 26, verses 39-44, "O my Father, if it be possible, let this cup pass from me: nevertheless not as I will, but as thou wilt." If it was recorded three times, He probably said the same prayer point many times. If Jesus Himself saw the need to repeat the same point as He battled with the bitter cup of our sins, how about us.

I am sure Jacob, as he wrestled with the angel, must have said, "I will not let you go till you bless me" several times. The same with the woman who had an issue of blood. How about blind Bartimaeus who hollered the same thing all day.

I have had people get baptized in the Holy Ghost for the first time because they said, "Thank you, Jesus" over and over till they broke into tongues. I will ask them to say, "Lord Jesus, baptize me in the Holy Ghost and with fire" a few times and just tell them to start thanking Jesus until they break into tongues. It almost always manifests.

"Fervent" means *showing ardent or extremely passionate enthusiasm.* I did not write the prayers that follow, but I have had miraculous breakthroughs in many aspects of my life praying such prayers—sometimes sticking to a point that touched my spirit or my personal circumstance many times till I felt a release.

In my experience and testimonies, I have had miraculous answers to prayer by lying on the floor and just saying, "Jesus help me" over and over. So you may choose to read the prayer as a novel or you can pray it with fervency knowing that the fervent, effectual prayers of the righteous make much power available.

BREAKTHROUGH PRAYERS

ADAPTED FROM THE WORKS OF

DR. D. K. OLUKOYA

Reprinted with permission

Pray these prayers as though your life depends on them, because it just may.

BREAKING THE MINISTERIAL CURSE OF FAILURE

Eph. 1:3-10

To deal with every conscious and unconscious curse of ministerial failure.

CONFESSIONS

I am a manifestation, the product and the result of God's word. God has spoken into my life and I have become the manifest presence of Jehovah God on earth. I expressly manifest everything the Word of God says I am. I am filled with the word of life.

The Word of God is in me, not written in ink, but by the spirit of the living God; not on table of stone, but on the flesh-table of the heart.

The Word of God in me is a quickening spirit and always keeping me alive.

I have received the body and the blood of Jesus Christ; I am full of Him. He is the bread of life sent from heaven. I have eaten Him, I shall not hunger or thirst or die because in Him is life, and life eternal.

I receive all the blessings that accompany the Word of God. I decree that they become operational in my life and I ask for a speedy physical manifestation of the results in my life.

I am not an image of failure, and I am not fashioned after the likeness of a god of the tail. I am the salt of the earth. On the inside of me is every excellence of the power of God. God has put this feature of His power in earthen vessels. This power is in me. My appearance is as the appearance of a horse. So I leap. I run like mighty men. When I fall upon the sword, it cannot hurt me. The Word of God has made me a brazen wall, a fortified city, an iron pillar. My presence terrifies the enemy. He trembles, feels much pain and travails at the sound of my voice which the Lord has empowered. For it is written, wherever the voice of the king is, there is authority.

With my heart I believe the power in the Word of God. With my mouth I have made confessions. Therefore as I go into prayer, let the word run swiftly to perform my requests and bring results, in the name of Jesus.

PRAISE WORSHIP

- *Yea, though I walk through the valley of the shadow of death, I will fear no evil: for Thou art with me; Thy rod and Thy staff they comfort me.* Every curse of untimely death operating in the lives of God's ministers, especially in this country; break and loose your hold over my life, in the name of Jesus.

- *Mark the perfect man, and behold the upright: for the end of that man is peace.* My calling shall not be aborted; I will complete my assignment with peace, in the name of Jesus.

- *For this God is our God for ever and ever. He will be our guide even unto death.* Every curse inspiring the ministers of God to leave His guiding light; I break you and loose myself from you, in the name of Jesus.

- *But God will redeem my soul from the power of the grave for He shall receive me.* Any power hunting to convert me to a living and walking corpse, fall down and perish, in the name of Jesus.

- *My flesh and my heart fail but God is the strength of my heart, and my portion for ever.* Any power feeding on the anointing and strength of God's minister, be consumed over my life, in the name of Jesus.

- *He will swallow up death in victory; and the Lord God will wipe away tears from off all faces; and the rebuke of His people shall He take away from off all the earth for the Lord has spoken it.* Let the precious blood of Jesus swallow every death sentence placed upon any member of my family, in the name of Jesus.

- *I will ransom them from the power of the grave; I will redeem them from death: O death, I will be thy plagues; O grave, I will be thy destruction; repentance shall be hid from mine eyes.* Every curse of death before success, every curse issued by occultists, witches, rulers of darkness and local wickedness against God's ministers in this country, I break you by the blood of Jesus over my life, in the name of Jesus.

- *But thou shall remember the Lord thy God: for it is He that giveth thee power to get wealth.* Every curse of financial failure and poverty, be destroyed by the blood of Jesus.

- *For the Lord thy God blesseth thee, as He promised thee: and thou shalt lend unto many nations, but thou shall not borrow.* Every curse of borrowing, lacking and wanting in the lives of God's ministers, I loose myself from your grip by fire, in the name of Jesus.

- *The Lord shall open unto thee His good treasure, the heaven to give the rain unto thy land in His season and to bless all the work of thine hand.* Any power shutting off good treasures of God from my life, fall down and perish, in the name of Jesus.

- *For the Lord God is a sun and shield: the Lord will give grace and glory; no good thing will He withhold from them that walk uprightly.* Anything in me repelling the good things promised by God to His own, come out by fire, in the name of Jesus.

- *That I may cause those that love me to inherit substance; and I will fill their treasures.* Any power in my family and locality creating difficulty for me in obtaining good substance, receive multiple destruction, in the name of Jesus.

- *For the love of money is the root of all evil: which while some coveted after, they have erred from the faith, and pierced themselves through with many sorrows.* Every attack and maneuver of mammon making God's ministers easily diverted from the true gospel, be frustrated in my life and calling, in the name of Jesus.

- *He that loveth silver shall not be satisfied with sliver; nor he that loveth abundance with increase.* Every seed of mammon making God's ministers to lust after money and run after gains, be uprooted from my life and die, in the name of Jesus.

- *Before destruction the heart of man is haughty, and before honor is humility.* Every curse of failure and destruction of the ministers of God prospering through pride, I destroy you in my life, in the name of Jesus.

- *Pride goeth before destruction and an haughty spirit before a fall.* Anything in my flesh putting up and exhibiting haughtiness against God and His people, die now, in the name of Jesus.

- *A man's pride shall bring him low: but honor shall uphold the humble in spirit.* Every attack, plot, scheme, device, maneuver and operation of the enemy to bring me low (into the valley), be divinely frustrated to nothingness, in the name of Jesus.

- *For by means of a whorish woman a man is brought to a piece of bread.* Every woman agent assigned as an open sepulcher to swallow me and my calling up, receive speedy judgment of destruction, in the name of Jesus.

- *Now the works of the flesh are manifest, which are these: adultery, fornication, uncleanness, lasciviousness…* Every work of the flesh being exploited by the enemy against my calling, die now, in the name of Jesus.

- *Now these things became our examples to the intent that we should not lust after evil things as they also lusted.* I receive a special grace of God that will enable me to escape ministerial pitfalls that swallowed the people before me, in the name of Jesus.

- Rejoice in the Lord always, for we can do all things through Christ who is our strength. Bless the Lord for all your answered prayers.

SPIRITUAL SANITATION

Matthew 21:12

Many Christians are suffering from ancestral burdens which hinder their spiritual growth. This program is designed:

To help you obtain freedom from ancestral yokes and burdens.

To clean up the unprofitable spiritual background militating against your physical and spiritual progress.

Jesus is always in the business of driving away all strange elements undertaking satanic and destructive transactions in the body, soul and spirit. He will do no less for you as you cry unto Him.

CONFESSION

If a man therefore purges himself from these, he shall be a vessel unto honour, sanctified, and meet for the master's use, and prepared unto every good work.   2 Tim. 2:21

PRAISE WORSHIP

- I release myself from every ancestral, demonic pollution, in the name of Jesus.

- I release myself from every demonic pollution emanating from my parents' religion, in the name of Jesus.

- I release myself from every demonic pollution emanating from my past involvement in any demonic religion, in the name of Jesus.

- I break and loose myself from every idol and related associations, in the name of Jesus.

- I release myself from every dream pollution, in the name of Jesus.

- Let every satanic attack against my life in my dreams be converted to victory, in the name of Jesus.

- Let all rivers, trees, forests, evil companions, evil pursuers, visions of dead relatives, snakes, spirit husbands, spirit wives, and masquerades manipulated against me in the dream be completely destroyed by the power in the blood of Jesus.

- I command every evil plantation in my life to come out with all your roots, in the name of Jesus! (*Lay your hands on your stomach and keep repeating the emphasized area.*)

- All evil strangers in my body, come out of your hiding places, in the name of Jesus.

- I disconnect any conscious or unconscious linkage with demonic caterers, in the name of Jesus.

- Let all avenues of eating or drinking spiritual poisons be closed, in the name of Jesus.

- I cough out and vomit any food eaten from the table of the devil, in the name of Jesus. (*Cough and vomit them out in faith. Prime the expulsion.*)

- Let all evil materials circulating in my bloodstream be evacuated, in the name of Jesus.
- I drink the blood of Jesus. (*Physically swallow and drink it in faith. Keep doing this for some time.*)
- Lay one hand on your head and the other on your stomach or navel and begin to pray like this: "Holy Ghost fire, burn from the top of my head to the soles of my feet." Begin to mention every organ of your body; your kidneys, liver, intestines, blood, etc. You must not rush at this level, because the fire will actually come and you may start feeling the heat.
- I cut myself off from every spirit of… (*mention the name of your place of birth*), in the name of Jesus.
- I cut myself off from every tribal spirit and curse, in the name of Jesus.
- I cut myself off from every territorial spirit and curse, in the name of Jesus.
- Holy Ghost fire, purge my life, in the name of Jesus.
- I claim my complete deliverance from the spirit of … (*mention those things you do not desire in your life*), in the name of Jesus.
- I break the hold of any evil power over my life, in the name of Jesus.
- Thank God for answers to your prayer.

WAR AGAINST ANTI-MARRIAGE FORCES

Mathew 19:6

When your marriage is being threatened...

One of the devices of the enemy to make people objects of ridicule is preventing them from getting married. You must take up all the armor of God to counter all the measures taken by the enemy to subject you to perpetual frustration.

Pray to God to give you true love for your spouse. Ask the Lord to teach you how to love your spouse and meet his/her needs (emotional, financial, material, physical, and spiritual).

The love you have for your spouse will cause you to continually intercede for him/her in prayer. These prayer points have been designed to destroy all anti-marriage forces. As you pray them from a heart of love, God will give you the victory.

CONFESSION

The pride of thine heart hath deceived thee, thou that dwellest in the clefts of the rock, whose habitation is high; that saith in his heart, who shall bring me down to the ground? Though thou exalt thyself as the eagle, and though thou set thy nest among the stars, thence will I bring thee down, saith the Lord.　　　　　　　　　　　　　Obad. 1:3-4

PRAISE WORSHIP

- All evil counsels against my marital life, collapse, in the name of Jesus.

- Any association between my husband/wife and any strange man/woman, be scattered now, in the name of Jesus.

- Every demonic in-law, loose your hold upon my life, in the name of Jesus.

- Spirit husbands and spirit wives, loose your hold, in the name of Jesus *(place your hand below your stomach)*.

- Every curse that has been issued against my marriage, be cancelled, in the name of Jesus.

- Every demonic mark contrary to settled homes, be wiped off with the blood of Jesus.

- Every inherited spirit that is not of God, go, in the name of Jesus.

- Every curse issued against my marriage or against my marital life, be broken, in the name of Jesus.

- Let the effect of every ceremony done on the day of my wedding, and which has been working against me, be cancelled and destroyed, in the name of Jesus.

- Every spiritual dowry collected on my behalf, I return you to the sender, in the name of Jesus.

- The spiritual marriage of my husband/wife to his/her mother, be dissolved, in the name of Jesus.

- Any power which says that I will not enjoy my marital life, be roasted, in the name of Jesus.

- I command my run-away husband/wife to come back, in the name of Jesus.
- You, spirit of marriage destruction, be bound, in the name of Jesus.
- I command every curse on my marriage to be converted to blessing, in the name of Jesus.
- I command every evil which strange friends have done against my home to be reversed, in the name of Jesus.
- I release my partner from every demonic cage, in the name of Jesus.
- Thank God for answers to your prayer.

SPIRITUAL GROWTH

John 3:30

For all believers who desire meaningful spiritual growth in their walk with God.

There is no height you cannot attain in the Spirit if only you are ready to take the bull by the horn; do away with every form of hindrance and follow the principles of spiritual growth laid down in God's Word.

For when for the time ye ought to be teachers, ye have need that one teach you again which be the first principles of the oracles of God; and are become such as have need of mild and not of strong meat. Hebrews 5:12

Jesus expects each believer to grow to the level where he/she can teach others. In many of the Epistles, the believer is encouraged to grow in grace and in the knowledge of Christ (2 Peter 3:18). When a believer refuses to grow, he/she remains a spiritual babe who is unskillful in the WORD. Such baby Christians need milk and not strong meat.

When we, as believers, begin to apply the truth we know in our lives, we will begin to grow and our knowledge of Christ will also increase. Paul encourages the believers to be "rooted and built up in Him" (Col. 2:7). As believers, we draw our nutrients from Him, i.e., Jesus Christ.

As you pray these prayer points for spiritual growth, the Holy Spirit will draw you into a deeper and more fulfilling relationship with Christ.

SCRIPTURE FOR MEDITATION

That I may know Him, and the power of His resurrection and the fellowship of His sufferings, being made conformable unto His death;... I press toward the mark for the prize of the high calling of God in Christ Jesus. Phil. 3:10, 14

Make the following confessions to establish your identity in Christ Jesus:

I am not what the world thinks or says I am. I am not what the devil or the kingdom of darkness says, imagines or has designed me to be. I am not the picture of what my idolatrous forefathers wished I would be. I am not what the unregenerated minds of my friends think I am. I am not what my father and mother think or want me to be. I am not what my village wickedness, household wickedness and environmental wickedness want me to be. I am not a picture of what the national economy and institutionalized wickedness have restructured the people to be. I am not what I think I am.

I am what the Word of God says I am. I am an express image of Jehovah God on earth. I am fashioned after the likeness of the Creator of the heavens and earth. I am regenerated by the blood of Jesus. I am ransomed from the powers of death and hell. I am blood-washed. I am redeemed. I am justified by Christ. I am made to be the righteousness of God through Christ. I am a believer of the word of truth. I am born again. I am heaven-bound; my citizenship is in heaven. I am seated with Christ in heavenly places, far above principalities and powers. I am a priest and a king ordained by Christ to rule here on earth. I am the fear and the dread of God against the kingdom of darkness. I am a dwelling place of the Holy Spirit of God. I am built up together and attached with other children of God into a holy habitation of God.

The Word of God says I am a royal priesthood. I am a holy nation. I am a chosen generation and a peculiar person to the nation. I am special in the sight of God. The Bible says because I believe and receive Jesus Christ, power has been given to me to become a son of God. I am empowered to trample upon serpents and scorpions and all the powers of the enemy. I am empowered to use the name of Jesus to cast out demons and heal the sick. I am empowered to bind, to loose, and to decree things; and the Bible says wherever my voice is heard, no one can ask me why. I do these things, for my voice is the voice of a king that is full of authority.

I am commanded and empowered by my God to subdue and to exercise dominion; for I am made a little lower than the angels, and God has crowned me with glory and honor and has also made me to have dominion over all the works of His hands. The devil that was against my authority as God's representative on earth has been destroyed by Christ. And once again the keys of the kingdom of heaven are given to me and because I am a member of the body of Christ, which is the church, the gates of hell cannot prevail against me.

I am a branch in the vine; Jesus Christ is the true vine because I abide in Him. I am full of the fruit of the Spirit. I am full of love, joy, peace, longsuffering, kindness, goodness, faithfulness, gentleness, self control. Because the grace of God is upon my life as the light of His glory, I am full of divine favor; I am a partaker of all of heaven's spiritual blessings.

I am an over-comer; the Bible says whosoever is born of God overcomes the world, and this is the victory that overcomes the world, even my faith. In faith I overcome ungodly worry, anxiety, heaviness of spirit, sorrow, depression, lust of the eyes and lust of the flesh. In faith I have overcome all the tricks of the devil; for it is written, greater is Jesus Christ that dwells in me than the devil that is in the world. No weapon that is formed against me shall prosper. In righteousness I am established. I am far from oppression, for I shall not fear from terror. It shall not come near me. The Lord shall cover me with His feathers, because I have made Him my dwelling place. Evil shall not befall me. I shall tread upon the lion and the cobra and surely the Lord will always deliver me from the snare of the fowler. God has made me a beneficiary of divine health through the stripes that were laid on Jesus Christ. Through Jesus Christ I have right standing with God. Through Jesus Christ I have access to the throne of grace of God, to find peace with God. I have prosperity, for God will no longer withhold any good thing from me.

I have spoken with the tongue of the learned, and as it is written, I shall be justified by the words of my mouth. I ask that the Word of God I have confessed begin to transform me to the original image God designed me to be in His book. I ask that the blood of Jesus wipe away every mark of reproach, whether physical or spiritual. I ask for the blood of Jesus to erase every evil and negative name I was ever called. I nullify every negative report ever made about me. I cease to be a picture of failure. I cease to be abased, rejected, forsaken, desolate and downcast. I begin to manifest, expressly, every good thing God has written about me in His book. I begin to look fearfully and wonderfully made. I begin to operate at the head and not the tail. I begin to be a true worshipper of Jehovah El Shaddai and I begin, from now, to continually praise Him and confess positively.

PRAISE AND WORSHIP

- Lord, comfort my heart.
- Lord, establish me in every good work.
- Lord, establish me in every good word.
- God of peace, sanctify me wholly, in the name of Jesus.
- Father Lord, let my body, soul and spirit be preserved blameless unto the coming of our Lord Jesus Christ, in the name of Jesus.
- Let me be filled with the knowledge of His will, in the name of Jesus.
- Let me be filled with all wisdom and spiritual understand-

ing, in the name of Jesus.

- Father Lord, help me to walk worthy of and pleasing to the Lord, in the name of Jesus.
- Father Lord, make me be fruitful in every good work, in the name of Jesus.
- Lord, increase me in the knowledge of God.
- Lord, strengthen me mightily.
- Father Lord, let me be filled with the spirit of wisdom and understanding in the knowledge of Christ, in the name of Jesus.
- Father Lord, let the eyes of my understanding be enlightened, in the name of Jesus.
- Father Lord, let me be strengthened with might by His spirit in the inner man, in the name of Jesus.
- Father Lord, let Christ dwell in my heart by faith, in the name of Jesus.
- Lord, let me be filled with all the fullness of God.
- God, help me comprehend the breadth, length, depth and height of the love of Christ, in the name of Jesus.
- Let the word of the Lord have free course and be glorified in me, in the name of Jesus.
- Let the Lord's peace give me peace in all areas of my life, in the name of Jesus.
- Let utterance be given unto me to make known the mystery of the Gospel, in the name of Jesus.
- Lord, perfect what is lacking in my faith.
- Lord, perfect Your good work in me.

- Lord, make me perfect unto Your good work.
- Lord, enrich me in all utterance and knowledge.
- Let the grace of the Lord Jesus Christ be with me, in the name of Jesus.
- Father Lord, inject into me your spiritual vitamins that will make me spiritually healthy, in the name of Jesus.
- Father Lord, inject into me spiritual vitamins that will boost my appetite to eat Your word, in the name of Jesus.
- Lord God, inject into me spiritual vitamins that will clear my vision and strengthen its clarity, in the name of Jesus.
- Lord God, inject into me spiritual vitamins that will sustain me in evil days.
- Lord God, inject into me divine immunity that will always kill spiritual germs and evil deposits in me.
- Lord God, inject into me the spiritual energy that will make me tireless with You.
- Lord God, feed me with the foods of champions.
- Lord God, boost my energy to run the race set before me.
- I receive the comforting anointing and power in the Holy Ghost, in the name of Jesus.
- I receive the unsearchable wisdom in the Holy Ghost, in the name of Jesus.
- I take the shield of faith to quench every fiery dart of the enemy, in the name of Jesus.
- I run into the name of the Lord which is a strong tower and I am safe, in the name of Jesus.
- Father Lord, always make me drink from Your everlasting

well of joy, in the name of Jesus.

- Thank God for the new spiritual height to which He has lifted you.

DELIVERANCE FROM FOUNDATIONAL BONDAGE

Psalm 11:13

This is recommended as the first series of prayers to be said during deliverance sessions:

To obtain deliverance from foundational contamination and bondage.

To release yourself from ancestral yokes and burdens.

To clean up any unprofitable spiritual background militating against your physical and spiritual progress.

It will do you well, if you can agree with me that the problems of people stem from their foundations. Why not get up and get going and face it squarely in prayer, so that you can get out of the stigma.

"If the foundations be destroyed, what can the righteous do?"
Psalm 11:3

In architecture, the foundation is the most important part of a building. This is the part on which the whole building will rest. It has to be solid. The height of the building is determined by the foundation.

Where we get to in life depends on the kind of foundation we have. The ability to read is the foundation for further education. It is impossible for an illiterate to graduate from a university.

Many of us have foundations that will limit and hinder our physical and spiritual progress. Such foundations are the result of evil dedications and evil inheritances which have now become bondage, limiting success in life. The enemy of man's soul knows how to convert footholds into strongholds.

The good news is that as a believer, a born again, spirit-filled Christian, your foundation is Christ. The faulty foundation of your childhood can be repaired. As you use these prayer points, Christ Jesus will step into your life to rebuild every faulty foundation, and He will release you from every foundational bondage.

CONFESSIONS

Christ hath redeemed us from the curse of the law, being made a curse for us: for it is written, Cursed is everyone that hangeth on a tree: That the blessing of Abraham might come on the gentiles through Jesus Christ; that we might receive the promise of the spirit through faith. Gal. 3:13-14

I indeed baptize you with water unto repentance: but he that cometh after me is mightier than I, whose shoes I am not worthy to bear: he shall baptize you with the Holy Ghost, and with fire. Matt. 3:11

Who hath delivered us from the power of darkness, and hath translated us into the kingdom of his dear son.   Col. 1:13

And having spoiled principalities and powers, he made a shew of them openly, triumphing over them in it. Col. 2:15

And the Lord shall deliver me from every evil work, and will preserve me unto his heavenly kingdom; to whom be glory for ever and ever. Amen.   2 Tim. 4:18

And deliver them who through fear of death were all their life-time subject to bondage.   Heb. 2:1

When the wicked, even mine enemies and my foes, came upon me to eat up my flesh, they stumbled and fell.   Psalm 27:2

NOTE: Prayers of release from foundational bondage have to be said aggressively. No stone should be left unturned. You must hate foundational bondages with perfect hatred. Scriptural fasting will enhance deliverance.

PRAISE WORSHIP

- Thank you, God, for making provision for deliverance from any form of bondage.
- I confess my sins and those of my ancestors, especially those sins linked to evil powers.
- I cover myself with the blood of Jesus.

- I release myself from any inherited bondage, in the name of Jesus.
- Lord, send your axe of fire to the foundation of my life and destroy every evil plantation.
- Let the blood of Jesus flush out from my system every inherited satanic deposit, in the name of Jesus.
- Let the blood of Jesus and the fire of the Holy Ghost cleanse every organ in my body, in the name of Jesus.
- I break and loose myself from every inherited evil covenant, in the name of Jesus.
- I break and loose myself from every inherited evil curse, in the name of Jesus.
- I vomit every evil consumption that I have been fed with as a child, in the name of Jesus.
- I command all foundational strongmen attached to my life to be paralyzed, in the name of Jesus.
- Let any rod of the wicked rising up against my family line be rendered impotent for my sake, in the name of Jesus.
- I command all foundational strongmen attached to my life to be paralyzed, in the name of Jesus.
- I cancel the consequences of any evil local name attached to my person, in the name of Jesus.
- Pray aggressively against the following evil foundations. Pray as follows: You (*pick the under-listed, one by one*), loose your hold over my life and be purged out of my foundation, in the name of Jesus.
  - evil physical design

- parental curses
- envious rivalry
- demonic blood transfusion
- evil dedication
- demonic alteration of destiny
- demonic incisions
- demonic marriage
- dream pollution
- evil laying on of hands
- demonic sacrifice
- fellowship with family idols
- exposure to evil diviner
- inherited infirmity
- fellowship with local idols
- wrong exposure to sex
- destructive effect of polygamy
- demonic initiations
- unscriptural manner of conception
- fellowship with demonic consultants

- You evil foundational plantation, come out of my life with all your roots, in the name of Jesus.
- I break and loose myself from every form of demonic bewitchment, in the name of Jesus.
- I release myself from every evil domination and control, in the name of Jesus.
- Let the blood of Jesus be transfused into my blood vessel.

- Let every gate opened to the enemy by my foundation be closed forever with the blood of Jesus.
- Lord Jesus, walk back into every second of my life and deliver me where I need deliverance, heal me where I need healing, transform me where I need transformation.
- Lord Jesus, I thank You for this wonderful deliverance.

POWER AGAINST SATANIC COUNTERATTACK

Isaiah 59:19

CONFESSIONS

The Lord shall cause my enemies that rise up against me to be smitten before my face: they shall come out against me in one way, and flee before me seven ways.

For the Lord my God is He that goeth with me, to fight for me against my enemies to save me. They that hate me shall be clothed with shame; and the dwelling place of the wicked shall come to naught.

For in the time of trouble He shall hide me in His pavilion: in the secret of His tabernacle shall He hide me; He shall set me up upon a rock. And now shall mine head be lifted up above mine enemies round about me: therefore will I offer in His tabernacle sacrifices of joy.

Through God I shall do valiantly: for it is He that shall tread down my enemies.

For the rod of the wicked shall not rest upon the lot of the righteous; lest the plenteous put forth their hands unto iniquity.

I am not afraid of sudden fear, neither of desolation of the wicked when it cometh, for the Lord shall be my confidence and shall stop my foot from being taken. Behold all that are incensed against me shall be ashamed and confounded: they shall be as nothing: and they that strive with me shall perish. I shall seek them, and shall not find, even them that contend with me, they that war against me shall be as nothing, and as a thing of naught.

Behold they shall surely gather together, but not by me: whosoever shall gather against me shall fall for my sake. But I will deliver thee in that day, saith the Lord: and thou shall not be given into the hand of men of whom thou art afraid. For I will surely deliver thee, and thou shall not fall by the sword, but thy life shall be for a prey for thee; because thou has thy trust in me, saith the Lord.

And shall God not avenge his own elect which cry day and night unto him though he bear long with them?

The angel of the Lord encampeth round about them that fear Him and delivereth them.

For the Lord loveth judgment, and forsaketh not His saints; they are preserved forever, but the seeds of the wicked shall be cut off.

But the Lord is faithful, who shall stablish you, and keep you from evil.

For the eyes of the Lord are over the righteous, and His ears are open unto his prayers.

The Lord knoweth how to deliver the godly out of temptations and to reserve the unjust unto the day of judgment to be punished.

PRAISE WORSHIP

- I cover myself properly with the blood of Jesus and stand against any power that is ready to resist me.
- Any satanic agent pretending to be a counselee in order to

project evil into my life, be disgraced, in the name of Jesus.

- Any spiritual arrow I have prayed out of anybody that is now in my family, be roasted by fire, in the name of Jesus.

- Any demon of marital bondage the Holy Ghost has ever used me to cast out of people's marriages before, now oppressing my marriage, loose your hold by fire in the name of Jesus.

- Any demon of infirmity in my life or in my family as a result of my ministering to people possessed of it, get out now by fire, in the name of Jesus.

- Any household witchcraft the Holy Ghost has used my ministry to cast out, which is now affecting me or my family, be suddenly destroyed, in the name of Jesus.

- Any marine witchcraft rage against me and my family as a result of destroying their works in people's lives, be silenced by the blood of Jesus.

- Any member of my family being oppressed by any familiar spirit that was cast out through my ministry, receive divine deliverance, in the name of Jesus.

- Every spiritual wickedness in the heavenlies reinforcing against me and my ministry, be disgraced by the blood of Jesus.

- Every servient spirit assigned against me to be watching for my unguarded hour, receive thunderbolts of God and depart from me, in the name of Jesus.

- Every assembly of local witchcraft formed against my ministry, receive a baptism of multiple destruction, in the name of Jesus.

- Any power divining against me and my ministry, fall down and perish, in the name of Jesus.

- Any power circulating my name for evil as a result of my ministry work, fall down and die now, in the name of Jesus.

- Any satanic agent that is already in the sheepfold purposefully to watch and report me back to the evil world, be exposed and be disgraced, in the name of Jesus.

- Let every ministerial hazard I have ever suffered be healed by the blood of Jesus.

- Every good thing carted away by raging demons from my marriage, financial life and ministry, be restored a hundredfold, in the name of Jesus.

- Any demon assigned to be frustrating my success at the edge of breakthroughs, depart by fire in the name of Jesus.

- Any power creating difficulties for me in ministry, be roasted by fire, in the name of Jesus.

- Any power creating disfavor and diverting my divinely appointed helpers, be suddenly destroyed, in the name of Jesus.

- Every arrow I have ever fired out that was returned to me, go back with a hundred-fold strength, in the name of Jesus.

- I shield myself with the blood of Jesus against any evil reunion, re-gathering, reattaching, and reinforcement, in the name of Jesus.

- Affliction shall not arise a second time in my life, in the name of Jesus.

- Henceforth, let no principality, power, ruler of darkness, spiritual wickedness in the heavenlies and local wickedness trouble me, for I bear in my body the marks of the Lamb of God.

ATTACKING THE ENEMY OF YOUR CALLING

Isaiah 59:19

This prayer is specifically designed for ministers. To be used when:

Things are not moving in your ministry.

There is a satanic gang-up in your ministry.

Your ministerial life is being attacked by disappointments, frustrations, and division.

Signs and wonders completely elude your ministry.

You are unable to focus your attention on what God expects you to do.

You want to sharpen your spiritual sword.

CONFESSION:

And I say also unto thee, that thou art Peter, and upon this rock I will build my church; and the gates of hell shall not prevail against it. Matt. 16:18

PRAISE AND WORSHIP

- I destroy the power of every satanic arrest in my life, in the name of Jesus.

- All satanic arresting agents, release me, in the name of Jesus.

- I command every spiritual contamination in my life to receive cleansing by the blood of Jesus.
- Let the brush of the Lord scrub out every dirt in my spiritual pipe, in the name of Jesus.
- I destroy everything that is representing me in the demonic world with the fire of God, in the name of Jesus.
- Lord, teach me to die to self.
- Every rusted spiritual pipe in my life, receive wholeness in the name of Jesus.
- I command every power eating up my spiritual pipe to be roasted, in the name of Jesus.
- Spirit of the living God, quicken the whole of my being, in the name of Jesus.
- I command every hole in my spiritual pipe to be closed, in the name of Jesus.
- Lord God, stretch me and renew my strength, in the name of Jesus.
- Holy Spirit, open my eyes to see beyond the visible and make the invisible real to me, in the name of Jesus.
- Lord, ignite my calling with Your fire.
- Let my spiritual pipe receive the strength of God against any contamination, in the name of Jesus.
- Holy Spirit, open my eyes and let me have a revelation vision of Christ, in the name of Jesus.
- Lord, liberate my spirit to follow the leading of the Holy Spirit.
- I receive heavenly flushing in my spiritual pipe, in the name of Jesus.

- I confess that my spiritual pipe shall be effective throughout my life, in the name of Jesus.
- Holy Spirit, teach me to pray through problems instead of praying about them, in the name of Jesus.
- Lord, deliver me from the lies I tell myself.
- Every evil spiritual padlock and chain hindering my spiritual growth, be roasted, in the name of Jesus.
- I rebuke every spirit of spiritual deafness and blindness in my life, in the name of Jesus.
- Lord, deliver me from the lies the enemy tells me.
- Lord, empower me to resist Satan so that he would flee from me.
- I bind the strongman behind my spiritual blindness and deafness and paralyze his operations in my life, in the name of Jesus.
- I anoint my eyes and ears with the blood of Jesus.
- I choose to believe the report of the Lord and no other, in the name of Jesus.
- Let the fire of the Holy Spirit melt my resistance, in the name of Jesus.
- Lord, anoint my eyes and my ears that they may see and hear wondrous things from heaven.
- Let the fire of the Holy Spirit smash my pride, in the name of Jesus.
- Lord, anoint me to pray without ceasing.
- I send the fire of God to my eyes and ears to melt away every satanic deposit, in the name of Jesus.

- Let my spiritual eyes and ears be wide open, in the name of Jesus.
- In the name of Jesus, I capture every power behind all my spiritual blindness and deafness.
- Let my spiritual sight and hearing drum receive healing, in the name of Jesus.
- Holy Spirit, rain on me now, in the name of Jesus.
- Holy Spirit, uncover my darkest secrets, in the name of Jesus.
- You spirit of confusion, loose your hold over my life, in the name of Jesus.
- In the power of the Holy Spirit, I defy Satan's power, in the name of Jesus.
- Holy Spirit, pour Your healing power on me, in the name of Jesus.
- Let the water of life flush out every unwanted stranger in my life, in the name of Jesus.
- You enemies of the gospel in my life, be paralyzed, in the name of Jesus.
- Lord, begin to clean away from my life all that does not reflect You.
- Lord Jesus, nail me to Your cross.
- I reject every spiritual pollution, in the name of Jesus.
- Lord Jesus, break me, melt me, mold me, fill me and use me by the power of Your Spirit.
- Lord, I lose myself in You.

- Holy Spirit fire, ignite me to the glory of God, in the name of Jesus.
- Lord, let the anointing of the Holy Spirit break every yoke of backwardness in my life, in the name of Jesus.
- Let my spirit-man become divine fire, in the name of Jesus.
- I frustrate every demonic arrest over my spirit-man, in the name of Jesus.
- Let the blood of Jesus remove any retrogressive label from every area of my life, in the name of Jesus.
- All anti-breakthrough decrees, be revoked, in the name of Jesus.
- Holy Ghost fire, destroy every satanic garment in my life, in the name of Jesus.
- Lord, give unto me the key to good success, so that anywhere I go, the doors of prosperity will be opened unto me.
- Let every wicked house constructed against me be demolished, in the name of Jesus.
- Let the road close against every unprofitable visitation in my life, in the name of Jesus.
- Lord, establish me as a holy person unto You.
- Lord, let the anointing to excel in my spiritual and physical life fall on me.
- I shall not serve my enemies; my enemies shall bow down to me, in the name of Jesus.
- I bind every desert and poverty spirit in my life, in the name of Jesus.

- I reject the anointing of non-achievement in my handiwork, in the name of Jesus.
- I pull down all strongholds erected against my progress, in the name of Jesus.
- I recall all my blessings thrown into the water, the forest and any satanic bank, in the name of Jesus.
- Holy Spirit, control my ability to frame my words, in the name of Jesus.
- I cut down the roots of all problems in my life, in the name of Jesus.
- Let all satanic scorpions be rendered sting-less in every area of life, in the name of Jesus.
- Let all demonic serpents be rendered harmless in every area of my life, in the name of Jesus.
- I declare with my mouth that nothing shall be impossible with me, in the name of Jesus.
- Let the camp of the enemy be put in disarray, in the name of Jesus.
- Spiritual parasites in my life, be disgraced, in the name of Jesus.
- Let all my Herods receive spiritual decay, in the name of Jesus.
- Lord, let Your favor and that of man encompass me this year, in the name of Jesus.
- Let all evil worms in any area of my life die, in the name of Jesus.
- I reject any demonic limitation on my progress, in the name of Jesus.

- Let all evil handwritings against me be paralyzed, in the name of Jesus.
- I reject the spirit of the tail, and I choose the spirit of the head, in the name of Jesus.
- Let all those circulating my name for evil be disgraced, in the name of Jesus.
- Lord, put into my hand the gift that will elevate my calling, in the name of Jesus.
- Let all evil friends make mistakes that will expose them, in the name of Jesus.
- I will not lose my calling, in the name of Jesus.
- Let the strongmen from both sides of my family destroy themselves, in the name of Jesus.
- Lord, teach me to be crucified with You.
- Let not Your peace depart from me, O Lord.
- I command every blockage in my spiritual pipe to be cleared, in the name of Jesus.
- I refuse to wear the garment of tribulation and sorrow, in the name of Jesus.
- Let every rebellion flee from my heart, in the name of Jesus.
- Lord, let the spirit that flees from sin incubate my life.
- Let the secrets of hidden and open enemies be revealed, in the name of Jesus.
- I claim all of my rights now, in the name of Jesus.
- I command every satanic net to receive destruction, in the name of Jesus.

- Holy Ghost, grant me a glimpse of Your glory now, in the name of Jesus.
- Lord, create in me a clean heart by Your power.
- Lord, renew a right spirit within me.
- Holy Ghost, pour the Father's jealousy upon me now, in the name of Jesus.
- I renounce all rights to anger, in the name of Jesus.
- Holy Ghost, quicken me, in the name of Jesus.
- Lord, remove from me every root of irritation that keeps anger alive in me.
- Holy Ghost breathe on me now, in the name of Jesus.
- I reject all thoughts that I will never change, in the name of Jesus.
- Holy Ghost, fill me that I might bring forth healing power, in the name of Jesus.
- Lord, produce in me the power of self-control and gentleness.
- Lord, I thank You for promoting me.

FREEDOM FROM INORDINATE AFFECTIONS AND SOUL-TIES

Gal. 5:24

People who maintain that nobody can be free from willful sin or ties with the demonic world are ignorant of God's provision to set man free and make him free indeed. Appropriate this provision for your life by ensuring that you crucify your flesh with all its affections and lusts today.

CONFESSION

Gal. 6:17

PRAISE AND WORSHIP

- Thank you, Lord, for your redemptive power.
- I confess all of my sins and I ask for forgiveness.
- I release myself from all unprofitable friendships, in the name of Jesus.
- I come against the dark powers which have manipulated my friendship with…(*mention the name of the person*) and I break their powers over my life, in the name of Jesus.
- I bind all demonic authorities which motivated and con-

trolled my relationship with…(*mention the name of the person*) and I break their authority and power over my affections, in the name of Jesus.

- I command all evil "remote controllers" to loose their hold upon my affections, in the name of Jesus.
- I release myself from the hold of every bewitched relationship, in the name of Jesus.
- By the blood of Jesus, I remove myself from any strange authority ever exercised over me.
- I remove all evil soul-ties and affections, in the name of Jesus.
- I come against every desire and expectation of the enemy to engage me in any unprofitable relationship, in the name of Jesus.
- I break every ungodly relationship, in the name of Jesus.
- I break and renounce evil soul-ties I have had or may have had with:
  - Secret societies
  - Cults
  - Adulterers
  - Family members
  - Close friends
  - Organizations
  - Husbands
  - Past or present friends
  - Acquaintances
  - Wives

- ■ Engagements
- ■ Doctors
- ■ Clubs
- ■ Religious leaders
- ■ Social organizations
- ■ Preachers, etc.

- I renounce all hidden evil soul-ties, in the name of Jesus.
- I renounce, break and loose myself from all demonic subjection to any relationship, in the name of Jesus.
- I break all evil soul-ties and wash them away with the blood of the Lord Jesus.
- I remove myself from any strange authority exercised over me, in the name of Jesus.
- I remove all mind controlling manipulations between me and my friends or family members, in the name of Jesus.
- I claim deliverance from any negative affection towards anyone, in the name of Jesus.
- Let evil affections towards me be wiped off the mind of... (*mention the name of the person*), in the name of Jesus.
- Lord Jesus, I give You my affections, emotions and desires and I request that they be in submission to the Holy Spirit.
- Praise the Lord for answered prayer.

VICTORY IN THE HUMAN COURT

Isa. 54:15

When you want court cases decided in your favor.

When you have a court case.

When you face a panel which decides your fate.

When you dream of being convicted in a courtroom.

When there is a conspiracy against you and you need God's intervention.

As you pray these prayer points sincerely, God will cause the judge/magistrate to give a judgment that favors you.

CONFESSIONS

What shall we then say to these things? If God be for us, who can be against us? He that spared not His own Son, but delivered Him up for us all; how shall He not with Him also freely give us all things? Who shall lay anything to the charge of God's elect? It is God that justifieth. Who is he that condemneth? It is Christ that died, yea rather, that is risen again, who is even at the right hand of God, who also maketh intercession for us…Nay, in all these things we are more than conquerors through Him that loved us. Rom. 8: 31-34, 37

The LORD is my light and my salvation; whom shall I fear? The LORD is the strength of my life, of whom shall I be afraid? When the wicked, even mine enemies and my foes, came upon me to eat up my flesh, they stumbled and fell.

Psalm 27:1-2

For the Lord God will help me; therefore shall I not be confounded: therefore have I set my face like a flint, and I know that I shall not be ashamed. Isaiah 50:7

As it is written; Behold, I lay in Sion a stumbling stone and rock of offence: and whosoever believeth on Him shall not be ashamed. Rom. 9:33

But the LORD is with me as a mighty terrible one: therefore my persecutors shall stumble, and they shall not prevail: they shall be greatly ashamed; for they shall not prosper: their everlasting confusion shall be greatly ashamed; for they shall not prosper: their everlasting confusion shall never be forgotten.

Jer. 20:11

There are many devices in a man's heart; nevertheless the counsel of the LORD, that shall stand. Prov. 19:21

He disappointeth the devices of the crafty, so that their hands cannot perform their enterprise. Job 5:12

The king's heart is in the hand of the LORD, as the rivers of water: he turneth it whithersoever he will. Prov. 21:1

The earth is the LORD's and the fullness thereof; the world, and they that dwell therein. For He hath founded it upon the seas, and established it upon the floods. Psalm 24:1-2

NOTE: These prayers will only work for those who are on the right path of justice. It will not work for purposes that are unscriptural. However, an ignorant offender may find help from using the prayers.

PRAISE AND WORSHIP

- Thank you, Lord, because you are the Lord of hosts and the Man of war.
- I claim victory over every adversary in this court case, in the name of Jesus.
- I bind and paralyze the strongman employed or delegated to disgrace me, in the name of Jesus.
- Let all the affairs of my life be too hot for any evil power to manipulate, in the name of Jesus.
- Lord, grant me and my lawyer supernatural wisdom to subdue all opposition.
- Lord, let it be impossible for my adversary to subdue the truth in this matter, in the name of Jesus.
- Lord, let me find favor in the sight of those who are responsible for judging this case.

- I close every negative door that the enemy might want to open, using this case, in the name of Jesus.

- You satanic agents, I command you to clear out from the pathway to my victory in this matter, in the name of Jesus.

- I cancel any demonic decision and expectation concerning this case, in the name of Jesus.

- Father, make it possible for me to find favor in the sight of the judge, in the name of Jesus.

- Lord, let me find favor, compassion and loving-kindness with the jury, in the name of Jesus.

- Let all the demonic obstacles that have been established in the heart of anyone against my prosperity be destroyed, in the name of Jesus.

- Lord, give to all the parties concerned dreams, visions and restlessness that would advance my cause.

- I command my money being caged by the enemy to be completely released, in the name of Jesus.

- I bind and put to flight all the spirits of fear, anxiety and discouragement, in the name of Jesus.

- Lord, let divine wisdom fall upon all who are supporting me in these matters.

- I break the backbone of the spirits of conspiracy and treachery, in the name of Jesus.

- Lord, hammer my matter into the mind of those who will assist me so that they do not suffer from demonic loss of memory.

- I paralyze the handiwork of household enemies and envious agents in this matter, in the name of Jesus.

- You devil, take your leg away from the top of my finances, in the mighty name of Jesus.

- Let the fire of the Holy Spirit purge my life from any evil mark put upon me, in the name of Jesus.

- Let the Lord confuse the tongues of those gathered to do me harm, after the order of the builders of the Tower of Babel, in the name of Jesus.

- Let my adversaries make mistakes that will advance my cause, in the name of Jesus.

- I command every evil power and vessel sitting on my rights and goodness to be violently overthrown, in the name of Jesus.

- I pursue, overtake and recover my properties from the hands of spiritual Egyptians, in the name of Jesus.

- Let every counsel, plan, desire, expectation, imagination, device and activity of the enemy against this case be rendered null and void, in the name of Jesus.

- I terminate every journey into bondage and unfruitfulness designed for me by the enemies of my soul, in the name of Jesus.

- I bind every money-consuming demon attached to my finances, in the name of Jesus.

- I refuse to be tossed about by any demonic device of the enemy to delay my miracle, in the name of Jesus.

- Holy Spirit, teach me to avoid unfriendly friends and unprofitable transactions, in the name of Jesus.

- Let all my blessings presently in the prison of the enemy

begin to pursue me and overtake me as from today, in the name of Jesus.

- Begin to thank God for the victory.

WEALTH MUST CHANGE HANDS

2 Kings 7

For abundance, prosperity and financial breakthroughs.

To release wealth into your bosom.

To paralyze the spirit of poverty.

To recover lost benefits.

As you pray these prayer points, God will baptize you with the power to get wealth, and wealth will change hands in your life.

CONFESSIONS

For the LORD God is a sun and shield: the LORD will give grace and glory: no good thing will He withhold from them that walk uprightly. O LORD of hosts, blessed is the man that trusteth in thee. Psalm 84:11-12

But thou shalt remember the LORD thy God: for it is He that giveth thee power to get wealth, that He may establish His covenant which He sware unto thy fathers, as it is this day. Deut. 8:18

PRAISE WORSHIP

- Lord, let my Jacob become Israel today.
- Let my bald Samson begin to grow hair now, in the name of Jesus.
- Let every evil conspirator gathering against me be disbanded by fire, in the name of Jesus.
- Let evil vows against my future be rendered null and void, in the name of Jesus.
- You powers that quench the fire of God in one's life, I am not your candidate, in the name of Jesus.
- Every deeply-rooted problem in my life, be uprooted by fire, in the name of Jesus.
- I reject every evil domination and bondage in my life, in the name of Jesus.
- My angel of blessings will locate me today, in the name of Jesus.
- My angel of blessing will not go unless he blesses me, in the name of Jesus.
- Lord, let my cries provoke angelic assistance today.
- Lord, give me the name that will bless me today.
- Let every satanic hindrance targeted against my angel of blessing be dissolved by fire, in the name of Jesus.
- Lord, deliver me from evil stones thrown at me by unfriendly friends.
- Every evil riot and rage against me, be disgraced, in the name of Jesus.
- Lord, deliver me from every satanic noise.

- Lord, deliver me from the tumult of the people.
- Let every evil crowd seeking to take my life be scattered unto desolation, in the name of Jesus.
- Let all sicknesses come out with all their roots now, in the name of Jesus.
- Let the poison of sickness be drained out of my system now, in the name of Jesus.
- Let every abnormality within my body receive divine healing now, in the name of Jesus.
- Let every fountain of infirmity dry up now, in the name of Jesus.
- Every hunter of my health, be disappointed, in the name of Jesus.
- Let every stubborn pursuer of my health fall down and die now, in the name of Jesus.
- My head will not be anchored to any evil, in the name of Jesus.
- Let evil pursue all unrepentant evil workers, in the name of Jesus.
- I neutralize every power of tragedy, in the name of Jesus.
- No evil shall overtake me, in the name of Jesus.
- Every evil preparation against me, be frustrated, in the name of Jesus.
- Let every dead area of my blessings receive resurrection now, in the name of Jesus.
- Let the resurrection power of the Lord Jesus come upon the works of my hands now, in the name of Jesus.

- Lord, bless me to a dumbfounding degree.

- Lord, enlarge my coast.

- Let every embargo on my progress fall down and scatter, in the name of Jesus.

- I reject satanic restrictions in every area of my life, in the name of Jesus.

- Let the mighty hands of God be upon me for good, in the name of Jesus.

- Lord, keep me from all evil wisdom and manipulation.

- I reject any invitation to appointment with sorrow, in the name of Jesus.

- I scatter evil multitudes gathered against me, in the name of Jesus.

- Let God be God against my oppressors, in the name of Jesus.

- The Lord will not be a spectator in my affairs, but a participant, in the name of Jesus.

- Lord, save me from sinking in the sea of life.

- My head will not be anchored to doubt, in the name of Jesus.

- I refuse any evil diversion, in the name of Jesus.

- I will not take my eyes off the Lord Jesus, in the name of Jesus.

- Lord, anchor Your mercy to my head.

- Lord Jesus, let me receive the touch of signs and wonders now.

- Let God be God in my Red Sea situation, in the name of Jesus.

- God, let it be known that you are God in every department

of my life, in the name of Jesus.

- Lord, do a new thing to my enemies that will permanently dismantle their power.
- Lord, let uncommon techniques be utilized to disgrace any opposition against my life.
- Let the earth open up and swallow every stubborn pursuer in my life, in the name of Jesus.
- Lord God of Abraham, Isaac and Jacob, manifest Yourself in Your power to bless me.
- Lord, begin to answer every evil stronghold by fire and roast them to ashes.
- Every power challenging the power of God in my life, be disgraced now, in the name of Jesus.
- Let every rage of the enemy against my coming breakthroughs be disgraced now, in the name of Jesus.
- Let every evil imagination fashioned against me be frustrated and be disgraced by fire, in the name of Jesus.
- Let every satanic plan against my future glory be rendered as useless, in the name of Jesus.
- Evil rulers assembled against me, be scattered unto desolation, in the name of Jesus.
- Lord, behold the threatening of my enemies; give unto me divine boldness to prosper over them.
- Lord, stretch Your mighty hand to perform signs and wonders in my life.
- I speak destruction unto every desert spirit of poverty in my life, in the name of Jesus.

- I speak failure unto the spirit of impossibility in my life, in the name of Jesus.

- I speak disgrace unto the spirit of failure in my life, in the name of Jesus.

- Let every spirit of fruitlessness in my life be paralyzed now, in the name of Jesus.

- I reject every spirit of debt and bankruptcy in my life. Be paralyzed now, in the name of Jesus.

- Spirit of infirmity in my life, be paralyzed now, in the name of Jesus.

- Spirit of marriage destruction in my life, be paralyzed now, in the name of Jesus.

- Every desert security man assigned against my life, fall down and die now, in the name of Jesus.

- I release every faculty of my life from the dominion of desert spirits, in the name of Jesus.

- I paralyze the activities of desert spirits in my life, in the name of Jesus.

- Every evil load of desert spirits in my life, go back to your sender, in the name of Jesus.

- Every anointing of desert spirits upon my life, dry up by the fire of the Holy Ghost, in the name of Jesus.

- Blood of Jesus, block every doorway of poverty.

- All the powers assisting poverty in my life, be bound, in the name of Jesus.

- My life, receive the anointing of fruitfulness, in the name of Jesus.

- My life, refuse to be anchored to any evil, in the name of Jesus.
- My head, refuse to bear any evil burden, in the name of Jesus.
- I refuse to walk into any problem, in the name of Jesus.
- My hands, refuse to magnetize problems to me, in the name of Jesus.
- Every satanic architect of problems assigned against me, be roasted, in the name of Jesus.
- I break the backbone of any problem associated with every second of my life, in the name of Jesus.
- Any power that has been supplying strength to problems in my life, be wasted, in the name of Jesus.
- I refuse to swim in the ocean of problems in my life, in the name of Jesus.
- Every remotely controlled problem energized by household wickedness, be devoured by the Lion of Judah, in the name of Jesus.
- I sack and disband any power behind the problems in my life, in the name of Jesus.
- Lord Jesus, I refuse to be kept busy by the devil.
- I receive power to convert failures designed for my life to outstanding successes, in the name of Jesus.
- I receive power to close down every satanic factory designed for me, in the name of Jesus.
- Angels of blessings, begin to locate me for my own blessings in this program now, in the name of Jesus.

- Powers behind accidental problems, I am not your candidate. Fall down and die, in the name of Jesus.
- I receive the power to break every circle of problems, in the name of Jesus.
- Every attempt being made by destiny killers against my destiny, be frustrated unto death, in the name of Jesus.
- I command the fire of God to come upon every destiny killer working against my destiny, in the name of Jesus.
- I remove my destiny from the camp of destiny killers, in the name of Jesus.
- I use the fire of God and the blood of Jesus to surround my destiny, in the name of Jesus.
- Every power working against the fulfillment of my destiny, be disgraced, in the name of Jesus.
- I command my destiny to reject every bewitchment, in the name of Jesus.
- I deliver my destiny from the grip of destiny killers, in the name of Jesus.
- Every evil done to my destiny by household wickedness, be reversed now, in the name of Jesus.
- Every vessel of destiny killers fashioned against my destiny, fall down and die, in the name of Jesus.
- Let the ground open now and swallow all destiny killers working against me, in the name of Jesus.
- Every evil gathering against my destiny, be scattered, in the name of Jesus.

- My destiny, you will not manage poverty, in the name of Jesus.
- My destiny, you will not manage failure, in the name of Jesus.
- I command my destiny to begin to change to the best now, in the name of Jesus.
- My head will not carry evil loads, in the name of Jesus.
- Every enemy of progress in my life, fall down and die now, in the name of Jesus.
- I reject every evil manipulation against my destiny, in the name of Jesus.
- I paralyze every activity of destiny killers in every area of my life, in the name of Jesus.
- I smash every giant of "almost there" to pieces, in the name of Jesus.
- I destroy every castle of backwardness, in the name of Jesus.
- I receive the anointing to destroy every destiny killer, in the name of Jesus.
- Let every satanic guard organized against my life be paralyzed, in the name of Jesus.
- I frustrate every evil network designed against my life, in the name of Jesus.
- My enemies shall not understand the issues of my life, in the name of Jesus.
- My enemies shall not understand the issues of my finances and blessings, in the name of Jesus.

- Anything that has been done with a snail (*snail* here depicts a spirit, like stubborn as a mule and sly as a fox) to slow down my life, be destroyed by the blood of Jesus, in the name of Jesus.
- I reject every spirit of backwardness, in the name of Jesus.
- I reject caged life, in the name of Jesus.
- I reject caged finances, in the name of Jesus.
- I reject caged health, in the name of Jesus.
- I reject caged marriage, in the name of Jesus.
- I reject every spirit of stagnation, in the name of Jesus.
- Every satanic chain on my legs, break now, in the name of Jesus.
- Let every hole in my hands be blocked by the blood of Jesus, in the name of Jesus.
- My life shall not be hung on the shelf, in the name of Jesus.
- The hair of my Samson shall not be shaved, in the name of Jesus.
- Every anti-progress spirit, be bound by chains of fire, in the name of Jesus.
- Every satanic prison warden, fall down and die, in the name of Jesus.
- I shall not crash in the race of life, in the name of Jesus.
- My progress shall not be terminated, in the name of Jesus.
- Let my life be too hot for the enemy to handle, in the name of Jesus.
- Every power set up to pull me down spiritually, be disgraced, in the name of Jesus.

- Every power set up to pull me down physically, be disgraced, in the name of Jesus.

- Every power set up to pull my marriage down, be disgraced, in the name of Jesus.

- Every power set up to pull my finances down, be disgraced, in the name of Jesus.

- No "progress arrester" shall prevail over my life, in the name of Jesus.

- I receive power to excel in every area of my life, in the name of Jesus.

- I shall mount up on wings as the eagles, in the name of Jesus.

- I withdraw my wealth from the hand of the bondwoman and her children, in the name of Jesus.

- I will not squander my divine opportunities, in the name of Jesus.

- I must pray to get results in this program, in the name of Jesus.

- I dismantle any power working against my efficiency, in the name of Jesus.

- I refuse to lock the door of blessings against myself, in the name of Jesus.

- I refuse to be a wandering star, in the name of Jesus.

- I refuse to appear to disappear, in the name of Jesus.

- Let the riches of the Gentiles be transferred to me, in the name of Jesus.

- Let the angels of the Lord pursue every enemy of my prosperity to destruction, in the name of Jesus.
- Let the sword of the Goliath of poverty turn against himself, in the name of Jesus.
- Let wealth change hands in my life, in the name of Jesus.
- Lord, make a hole in the roof for me for my prosperity.
- Let the yoke of poverty upon my life be dashed to pieces, in the name of Jesus.
- Let every satanic siren scaring away my helpers be silenced, in the name of Jesus.
- Let every masquerading power swallowing my prosperity be destroyed, in the name of Jesus.
- Let every coffin constructed against my prosperity swallow the owner, in the name of Jesus.
- Let the ways of the evil angels of poverty delegated against me be dark and slippery, in the name of Jesus.
- Lord Jesus, hold my purse.
- Every demonic scarcity, be dissolved by fire, in the name of Jesus.
- By the wealthy name of Jesus, let heavenly resources rush to my door.
- I attack my lack with the sword of fire, in the name of Jesus.
- Satanic debt and credit, be dissolved, in the name of Jesus.
- Lord, be my eternal cashier.
- I bind the spirit of debt. I shall not borrow to eat, in the name of Jesus.

- Every evil meeting summoned against my prosperity, scatter without repair, in the name of Jesus.
- Every arrow of wickedness fired against my prosperity, be disgraced, in the name of Jesus.
- Let my life magnetize favor for breakthroughs, in the name of Jesus.
- I arrest every gadget of poverty, in the name of Jesus.
- I recover my blessings from any water, forest and satanic banks, in the name of Jesus.
- Let all my departed glory be restored, in the name of Jesus.
- Let all my departed virtues be restored, in the name of Jesus.
- Let God arise and let all my stubborn pursuers scatter, in the name of Jesus.
- Every attack by evil night creatures, be disgraced, in the name of Jesus.
- Let the wings of every spirit flying against me be dashed to pieces, in the name of Jesus.
- Angels of the living God, search the land of the living and the land of the dead and recover my stolen properties, in the name of Jesus.
- Every gadget of frustration, be dashed to pieces, in the name of Jesus.
- I break every curse of poverty working upon my life, in the name of Jesus.
- I bind every spirit drinking the blood of my prosperity, in the name of Jesus.

- Lord, create new and profitable opportunities for me.
- Let ministering angels bring customers and favor to me, in the name of Jesus.
- Anyone occupying my seat of prosperity, clear away, in the name of Jesus.
- Lord, make a way for me in the land of the living.
- I bind the spirit of fake and useless investments, in the name of Jesus.
- All unsold materials, be sold with profit, in the name of Jesus.
- Let all business failures be converted to success, in the name of Jesus.
- Every curse on my hands and legs, be broken, in the name of Jesus.
- Lord, embarrass me with abundance in every area of my life.
- Every effect of strange monies affecting my prosperity, be neutralized, in the name of Jesus.
- Let brassy heavens break forth and bring rain, in the name of Jesus.
- I break the control of every spirit of poverty over my life, in the name of Jesus.
- Lord Jesus, anoint my eyes to see the hidden riches of this world.
- Lord Jesus, advertise Your breakthroughs in my life.
- Let the riches of the ungodly be transferred into my hands, in the name of Jesus.

- I will rise above the unbelievers around me, in the name of Jesus.
- Lord, make me a reference point of divine blessings.
- Let blessings invade my life, in the name of Jesus.
- Let the anointing of excellence fall on me, in the name of Jesus.
- I disarm Satan as king and authority over my prosperity, in the name of Jesus.
- Let harvest overtake harvest in my life, in the name of Jesus.
- Let harvest overtake the sower in my life, in the name of Jesus.
- Every curse pronounced against my source of income, be broken, in the name of Jesus.
- Let my breakthroughs turn around for good, in the name of Jesus.
- Curses working against my destiny, break, in the name of Jesus.
- Lord, network me with divine helpers.
- Let life-transforming breakthroughs overtake me, in the name of Jesus.
- Let divine ability overtake me, in the name of Jesus.
- Lord, lead me to those who will bless me.
- Let my favor frustrate the plans of the enemy, in the name of Jesus.
- I will witness the downfall of my strongman, in the name of Jesus.

- I will be a lender and not a borrower, in the name of Jesus.
- My labor shall not be in vain, in the name of Jesus.
- Let embarrassing blessings overtake me in the name of Jesus.
- Lord, plant me by the rivers of prosperity.
- Unknown evil seeds in my life, I command you to refuse to germinate, in the name of Jesus.
- I refuse to get stuck on one level of blessing, in the name of Jesus.
- I shall possess all the good things I pursue, in the name of Jesus.
- Every effect of cursed house and load upon my prosperity, break, in the name of Jesus.
- Every power shielding me away from breakthroughs, fall down and die, in the name of Jesus.
- Let the garden of my life yield super abundance, in the name of Jesus.
- Every desert spirit, loose your hold upon my life, in the name of Jesus.
- Holy Spirit, plug my life into divine prosperity, in the name of Jesus.
- Every Achan in the camp of my breakthroughs, be exposed and be disgraced, in the name of Jesus.
- Every power operating demonic gadgets against my prosperity, fall down and die, in the name of Jesus.
- Every power passing evil current into my finances, loose your hold, in the name of Jesus.
- I break every circle of financial turbulence, in the name of Jesus.

- I smash the head of poverty on the wall of fire, in the name of Jesus.
- Ugly feet of poverty, walk out of my life now, in the name of Jesus.
- Every garment of poverty, walk out of my life now, in the name of Jesus.
- I reject financial burial, in the name of Jesus.
- Every garment of poverty, receive the fire of God, in the name of Jesus.
- I reject every witchcraft burial of my goodness, the name of Jesus.
- Woe unto every vessel of poverty pursuing me, in the name of Jesus.
- Let the fire of God burn away evil spiritual properties, in the name of Jesus.
- Poverty-identification marks, be rubbed off by the blood of Jesus.
- Lord, heal every financial leprosy in my life.
- Let my foundation be strengthened to carry divine prosperity, in the name of Jesus.
- Every stolen property and satanically transferred virtue, be restored, in the name of Jesus.
- Let every ordination of debt over my life be cancelled, in the name of Jesus.
- Lord, create newer and profitable opportunities for me.
- Every strange fire ignited against my prosperity, be quenched, in the name of Jesus.

- Let those sending my money to spiritual mortuary fall down and die, in the name of Jesus.

- Every power scaring away my prosperity, be paralyzed, in the name of Jesus.

- Every familiar spirit sharing my money before I receive it, be bound permanently, in the name of Jesus.

- Let every inherited design of poverty melt away by fire, in the name of Jesus.

- Let every evil rearrangement of prosperity be dismantled, in the name of Jesus.

- Lead me, O Lord, to my own land that flows with milk and honey.

- Let satanic giants occupying my Promised Land fall down and die, in the name of Jesus.

- Lord, empower me to climb my mountain of prosperity.

- Strongman of poverty in my life, fall down and die, in the name of Jesus.

- Spirits of famine and hunger, my life is not your candidate, in the name of Jesus.

- I remove my name from the book of financial embarrassment, in the name of Jesus.

- Every power reinforcing poverty against me, loose you hold, in the name of Jesus.

- I release myself from every bondage of poverty, in the name of Jesus.

- The riches of the Gentiles shall come to me, in the name of Jesus.

- Let divine magnets of prosperity be planted in my hands, in the name of Jesus.
- I retrieve my purse from the hand of Judas, in the name of Jesus.
- Let there be a reverse transfer of my satanically transferred wealth, in the name of Jesus.
- I take over the wealth of the sinner, in the name of Jesus.
- I recover the steering wheel of my wealth from the hands of evil diviners, in the name of Jesus.
- I refuse to lock the door of blessings against myself, in the name of Jesus.
- Lord, revive my blessings.
- Lord, return my stolen blessings.
- Lord, send God's angels to bring me blessings.
- Lord, let every thing that needs change in my life to bring me blessings be changed.
- Lord, reveal to me the key to my prosperity.
- Every power sitting on my wealth, fall down and die, in the name of Jesus.
- Lord, transfer the wealth of Laban to my Jacob.
- Let all those who hate my prosperity be put to shame, in the name of Jesus.
- Every evil bird swallowing my money, fall down and die, in the name of Jesus.
- Every arrow of poverty, go back to where you came from, in the name of Jesus.

- I bind every word spoken against my breakthroughs, in the name of Jesus.
- Every business house energized by Satan, fold up, in the name of Jesus.
- I destroy every clock and timetable of poverty, in the name of Jesus.
- Ever water spirit, touch not my prosperity, in the name of Jesus.
- Let men and women rush wealth to my doors, in the name of Jesus.
- I reject temporary blessings, in the name of Jesus.
- Every arrow of poverty energized by polygamy, fall down and die, in the name of Jesus.
- Every arrow of poverty energized by household wickedness, fall down and die, in the name of Jesus.
- Let power change hands in my finances, in the name of Jesus.
- Every serpent and scorpion of poverty, die, in the name of Jesus.
- I refuse to eat the bread of sorrow. I reject the water of affliction, in the name of Jesus.
- Let divine explosion fall upon my breakthroughs, in the name of Jesus.
- The enemy will not drag my finances on the ground, in the name of Jesus.
- Lord, advertise Your wealth and power in my life.
- Let promotion in my life, in the name of Jesus.
- I pursue and overtake my enemies and recover my wealth from them, in the name of Jesus.

- Holy Spirit, direct my hands into prosperity, in the name of Jesus.

USING THE BLOOD OF JESUS AS A WEAPON

2 Cor. 10:3-5

Regular prayers to overcome the satanic onslaught.

Deliverance prayers for stubborn cases.

The power for overcoming is in this blood.

These prayer points will teach you how to pray, using the blood of Jesus as a weapon.

CONFESSION

Rev. 12:11: *And they overcame him by the blood of the Lamb, and by the word of their testimony; as a weapon.*

In the name of Jesus Christ, I am a beloved child of God. I believe in God, I believe in Jesus Christ and I believe in the blessed Holy Spirit, Who is dwelling inside of me. I believe in the unshakeable and eternal power in the Word of God. I believe that life and death are in my tongue. I believe that as I make this confession unto life with the power in my tongue, according to the words which the Lord has this day put in my mouth, I shall prosper.

It is written that Jesus Christ offered His blood as a drink, and His flesh as bread that whosoever drinks and eats it shall not die forever. Now, with strong faith in my heart I hold in my hand a cup containing the blood of the Lamb of God and I drink it, that I may have life eternal.

I receive unto myself the virtues, strength, power, might and anointing in the blood. And I say: Let the blood quicken all that is dead within me. Let all sucked, sapped and paralyzed spiritual milk and strength of my life be resurrected by the blood. Let the blood re-energize, revitalize, reactivate and revive all dead potentials and spiritual gifts within me.

Let the blood flush out of me all inherited and self-acquired evil deposits in my system. Let it purify my blood system. Let it make old things pass away in my life and transform everything to become new. Let the power in the blood clean my spiritual vision and wash my spiritual pipe that I may be receiving of the Lord unhindered.

I eat with the heart of faith, the flesh of Jesus. For it is written, His flesh is bread indeed. I eat it now so that I can also eat with Him in His glory. I eat the flesh of Jesus to receive new spiritual strength and vigor; strength and vigor to put under subjection all works of the flesh; strength and vigor to paralyze the desires of my flesh; strength and vigor to paralyze the power of my flesh and make it obedient to the laws of the Lord.

As I eat and drink the flesh and blood of my Lord Jesus Christ, I renew my covenant with Him and I receive the life therein; for it is written, life is in the blood. Thus I possess the life and the spirit of Christ in me. Amen.

Jeremiah found the Word of God and did eat it, and it became the joy of his heart. I have found the Word of God and now, like vitamin pills, I throw it into my mouth and chew and digest it. Let it produce within me the power to rejoice in the Holy Ghost, the power to be steadfast in following God, the power to walk circumspectly, the power of holy living and the power of unashamed faithfulness in all circumstances.

The Word of God is spirit and it is life. It entered Ezekiel and he was put back on his feet. Let the Word of God raise up in me every downtrodden area of my life. Let the word, like fire, purify me and restore my parts stolen or destroyed by the enemy. Let the word build me up and give me inheritance amongst all sanctified brethren.

Let the joy of the Lord strengthen me. Let His right hand of righteousness uphold me. Let His countenance brighten up my life. Let the horn of His salvation lift me up out of the valley of life and let His living anointing oil fall on me like the dew of Hermon, and fill my life.

Lord, make me drunk with the blood of Jesus and I shall be full of life eternally.

Father Lord, as it is written, that I should be strong in the Lord and in the power of His might, I ask that You be my might and strength all the days of my life. Gird me with Your strength and let me not fall into the pit of enemies and I will praise You all the days of my life.

With my heart I believe the Word of God. With my mouth I have confessed unto salvation and justification. Oh Lord, let it be performed unto me as I have prayed, in Jesus Christ's only mighty name. Amen.

PRAISE WORSHIP

- Thank You, Father, for the benefits and provisions of the blood of Jesus.
- I stand on the ground of the blood of Jesus to proclaim victory over sin, Satan and his agents and the world.
- I apply the blood of Jesus to every stubborn problem in my life.
- I plead the blood of Jesus upon my body—from the top of my head to the soles of my feet.
- I soak my life in the blood of Jesus.
- I paralyze all satanic oppressors delegated against me with the blood of Jesus.
- I hold the blood of Jesus as a shield against any power that is already poised to resist me, in the name of Jesus.
- By the blood of Jesus, I stand against every device of distraction.
- I stand upon the Word of God and I declare myself unmovable, in the name of Jesus.
- Let every door that I have opened to the enemy be closed forever with the blood of Jesus.
- Make each of the following powerful confessions several times.
- Through the blood of Jesus, I have been redeemed out of the hands of the devil.
- I walk in the light, and the blood of Jesus cleanses me from all sins.
- Through the blood of Jesus, I have the life of God in me.

- Through the blood of Jesus, I have access to the presence of the Lord.
- I paralyze and cut off the head of Goliath with the blood of Jesus.
- If there is anything in me that is not of God, I don't want it. Depart, in the mighty name of Jesus.
- Let the blood of the Cross stand between me and any dark power delegated against me.
- I curse every work of darkness in my life to dry to the roots by the blood of Jesus.
- I defeat, paralyze and erase... (*pick from the under listed*) by the blood of Jesus
  - Spirit of demotion
  - Financial downgrading
  - Failure at the edge of miracle
  - Inherited problems
  - Vision killers
  - Dream attackers
  - Marital problems

- Let the power of the blood of Jesus be released on my behalf and let it speak against every dead bone in my life.
- Let the power of the blood of Jesus be released on my behalf and let it speak against every stubborn mountain in my life.
- In the name of Jesus, I plead the blood of Jesus.
- In the name of Jesus, I apply the blood of Jesus over my house.

- In the name of Jesus, I soak myself in the blood of Jesus.
- In the name of Jesus, I apply the blood of Jesus. Demons, you cannot re-enter my house.
- I draw a circle of the blood of Jesus around me.
- I draw the blood line of protection around my property.
- I overcome you, Satan, by the blood of the Lamb.
- You cannot put any sickness on me because I am redeemed by the blood of the Lamb.
- Let the blood of Jesus speak confusion into the camp of the enemy.
- Let the blood of Jesus speak destruction unto every evil growth in my life.
- Let the blood of Jesus speak disappearance unto every infirmity in my life.
- Let the blood of Jesus speak peace unto every broken marriage.
- Mr. Devil, see the blood of Jesus. The One who shed the blood crushed your head and He is my Lord.
- Let the blood of Jesus speak victory and prosperity unto my life.
- I sprinkle the blood of Jesus on all my properties.
- Let the blood of Jesus dry up every evil tree used against me.
- You evil power, I bring to bear the power of the blood of Jesus to bind you.
- I render every evil power militating against me impotent by the blood of Jesus.

- I hold the blood against you and declare that you have been defeated.
- Let the blood of Jesus minister defeat to every evil work in my life.
- Let the blood of Jesus bring down to nothing any evil work in my life.
- I minister death unto the enemy of progress in my life, by the blood of Jesus.
- I bind the staying power of any problem, by the blood of Jesus.
- I create a boundary against you devil, by the blood by Jesus.
- I hold the blood of Jesus against any evil spirit working against me.
- I hold the blood of Jesus against you, you spirit of... (*mention what is troubling you*). You have to flee.
- I enter the Holy of Holies by the blood of Jesus.
- I hold the blood of Jesus against the spirit of stagnation in any area of my life.
- I hold the blood of Jesus against demonic delay of my miracles.
- I hold the blood of Jesus against failure at the edge of success.
- I hold the blood of Jesus against the lack of good helpers.
- I hold the blood of Jesus against fruitless efforts in my life.
- I hold the blood of Jesus against occupying wrong positions.
- I hold the blood of Jesus against every delayed and denied promotion.

- I hold the blood of Jesus against dead accounts.
- I hold the blood of Jesus against evil diversion.
- I hold the blood of Jesus against lost foreign benefits.
- I hold the blood of Jesus against satanic prophecies.
- I hold the blood of Jesus against vagabond anointing.
- I hold the blood of Jesus against profit starvation.
- I hold the blood of Jesus against tortoise and snail anointing.

Fire Power, with Dr. Stella Gwandiku-Tita,
offers an extensive listing of prayer/teaching CD's that address
a variety of topics including:

"Get Out of Egypt"

"The Spirit of Prayer"

"Reclaiming Our Children"

"Contending for the Glory"

"Applying the Blood of Jesus"

"Healing from the Scriptures"

"Breaking Generational Curses"

"Removing the Curse of Poverty"

"Anti-Marriage Forces for Singles"

"Anti-Marriage Forces for Couples"

"Igniting the Fire of the Holy Ghost"

"Removing Hindrances at the Edge of Breakthroughs"

Dr. Stella Gwandiku-Tita is currently available for speaking
engagements and can be reached at:

Fire Power Ministry
P.O. Box 12788
Alexandria, LA 71315
(318) 792-5972

On the web: www.firepowerministries.com
Email:Firepowermins@aol.com